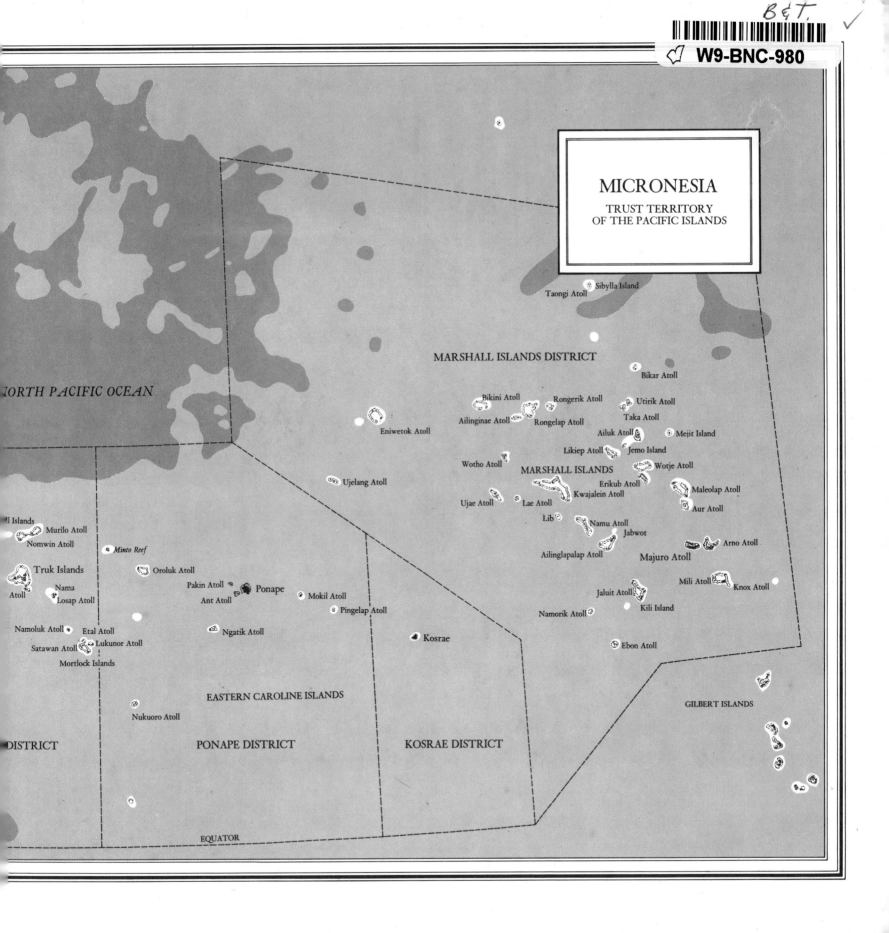

MICRONESIA

TRUST TERRITORY
OF THE PACIFIC ISLANDS

Taongi Atoll · Sibylla Island

MARSHALL ISLANDS DISTRICT

NORTH PACIFIC OCEAN

Bikar Atoll

Bikini Atoll · Rongerik Atoll · Utirik Atoll

Ailinginae Atoll · Rongelap Atoll · Taka Atoll

Eniwetok Atoll · Ailuk Atoll · Mejit Island

Wotho Atoll · Likiep Atoll · Jemo Island

MARSHALL ISLANDS

Ujelang Atoll · Erikub Atoll · Wotje Atoll

Kwajalein Atoll · Maleolap Atoll

Ujae Atoll · Lae Atoll · Aur Atoll

Lib · Namu Atoll

Jabwot

Arno Atoll

Ailinglapalap Atoll · Majuro Atoll

Mili Atoll · Knox Atoll

Jaluit Atoll

Kili Island

Namorik Atoll

Ebon Atoll

Murilo Atoll

Nomwin Atoll

Minto Reef

Truk Islands · Oroluk Atoll

Nama · Pakin Atoll · Ponape · Mokil Atoll

Losap Atoll · Ant Atoll · Pingelap Atoll

Namoluk Atoll · Etal Atoll

Satawan Atoll · Lukunor Atoll · Ngatik Atoll · Kosrae

Mortlock Islands

GILBERT ISLANDS

EASTERN CAROLINE ISLANDS

Nukuoro Atoll

DISTRICT · PONAPE DISTRICT · KOSRAE DISTRICT

EQUATOR

*Micronesia: the Land, the People and the Sea*

*Kenneth Brower*

# Micronesia

Louisiana State University Press, Baton Rouge and London

*Photographs by Harri Peccinotti*

# The Land, the People and the Sea

# Preface

There is certainly more to Micronesia than the image it conjures of tropical islands scattered over an expanse of ocean larger than the American Continent. Its name – which literally means tiny islands – is deceptive, but does not tell the whole story. Micronesia is in fact thousands of islands inhabited by diverse peoples – each with their own language, customs, and culture, and their own sense of community and political identity.

There are, however, certain unifying elements. One is the sea which paradoxically binds the islands even as it separates them. The sea is the common avenue for transport, trade, and social exchange among the islands. Because the sea has always been there, it has determined the livelihood, the crafts, and the legends of the peoples of Micronesia.

The islands also share the problem of preserving their colorful native lore and their way of life, as Micronesia is being discovered for its tourism potential and for its strategic location on the approaches to the Far East. The winds of modernization and change buffet its cultural preserves. Old ways are forgotten in favor of the new and foreign. Micronesia's precious little land is natural and unspoiled, but it is threatened by the exigencies of time and human needs.

Faced with incipient change, it is essential for Micronesians to have a record of the elements that comprise their indigenous culture. This book has been produced by Mobil Oil Micronesia as an expression of its long-term commitment to Micronesia and its appreciation of the culture of the islands.

J. P. Bailleux
*President,*
*Mobil Oil Micronesia Inc.*

# Foreword

Micronesia presents, in its 2,105 islands, contrasts and similarities often surprising to the outsiders. Stereotypes do not fit and yet there is a common underlying theme throughout. It is the size of the ocean and the minuscule nature of the islands on which people live.

Micronesians are little known. Their achievements are not the subject of extensive erudite academic research and their cultural history remains largely a mystery. And as with peoples all over the world, as change increases its tempo, old ways are displaced, lost and often forgotten. It is therefore most fortunate for us to have a book such as *Micronesia: the Land, the People and the Sea*. It is a book which honors the Micronesian traditional life style while recognizing changes that are inevitable to that life style. Mr. Brower, with an affectionate familiarity, recognizes the people's uniqueness, particularly their fishing and sailing skills and their ability to cope with the omnipresent sea.

As the various peoples of the Micronesian Islands increase their participation in a rapidly changing global environment, Mr. Brower's nostalgic revery and Mr. Peccinotti's outstanding photographs present a delightful introduction to how things used to be on the islands not too long ago.

We congratulate Mobil Oil Micronesia, Inc. for contributing this book on our Micronesian heritage.

Adrian P. Winkel
*High Commissioner,*
*Trust Territory of the Pacific Islands,*
*March 17 1981*

# Introduction

The dark hardwood of the hotel bar had been finished with epoxy, which gave it a permanent shine. The bar's surface was smooth and cool under the hand, and the light reflecting from it was easy on the eyes. Beyond, the noon sun was fierce on the reef and ocean, but here, under the lofty, mock-traditional roof of thatch, the day was pleasantly dim. The blue glint of the gin was wonderful in my glass. The lemon peel suspended there seemed the essence of gentility, a yellow slice from the very core of civilization.

At the hotel bars I knew best in Micronesia, you drank Budweiser in cans or scotch from plastic tumblers, and the brown barmaids wore expressions of monumental boredom, and the jukebox thundered Country-and-Western tunes. I'm not sure I don't like that gritty sort of hotel better, but this kind was nice for a change. Here no jukebox strummed *Okie from Tuskogee* or *Coward of the County*. There was no jukebox at all. The open-air bar was nearly empty. The only sounds were the hushed conversation from the only occupied table and the stirrings of the sea breeze in the palms of the slope below.

The place was Ponape, a big, green mountain-island in eastern Micronesia, and the hotel was called *The Village*. The Village's thatch-walled, thatch-roofed cottages were scattered, villagelike, through the green jungle of the slope.

Swivel-mounted on the terrace rail was a pair of massive binoculars. I had not seen binoculars like that since I was a boy on the San Francisco waterfront. There, you put a nickel in and swung them like a periscope on line with Alcatraz. The island was a penitentiary then, and you tried to imagine what life was like behind those rows of magnified but faceless windows. Here the binoculars were free. I walked to the railing. In the middle distance of the fringing reef, I saw, with unaided eyes, the dot of a human being moving. I swiveled the binoculars in the direction of the dot and pressed my eyes into the eyepieces.

I had an enlightenment. It was the literal sort of enlightenment that comes to the movie Dorothy when, transported by tornado in black-and-white from Kansas, she opens her door on the Technicolor land of Oz. The blued glass of the binoculars opened out on another world.

View from the Village Hotel, Ponape,
Federated States of Micronesia.

The realm beyond the lenses was charged with light and larger than life. That world of sunlight, I was instantly certain, was a real world, and this shadowy world of the hilltop bar – the blue of the gin, the wooden blades of the electric fans revolving slowly in the rafters, the glassy finish on the hardwood – was all a species of illusion. It was like looking out from a dream.

The moving dot on the fringing reef was a brown-black boy hunting fish. Across his shoulders was a pole, and from it dangled his catch. In his right hand was a stick. The binoculars brought him so close I could check the fit of the dark-blue shorts he was wearing. The shorts were too big for him. They hung low on his hips, and the white band of his underpants was showing. That white band was dazzling.

Micronesia absorbs more solar energy than any other place on earth, and everything below me was refulgent – the white elastic of the underpants, the beige-and-turquoise plain of the near reef, the white surf breaking on the far reef. The boy shimmered a little, for the air between us was super-heated by the sun and condensed by the binoculars. He was about 11. He was talking, I saw now, to another boy. The second boy was crouching and stationary, and I had missed him with my naked eye. The distance between them, foreshortened by the binoculars, was difficult to judge, but I guessed they were about 50 feet apart. While I watched, the standing boy used his stick as a crowbar to turn a coral stone. He peered under it, saw nothing of interest there, and moved on toward his friend.

Through the binoculars, the reef flat seemed enormous. When I lost the figures of the boys, I had trouble finding them again. Searching, the binoculars wandered endlessly over the bright, shallow-water plain that fringed the island. Those parts of the reef that were high and dry, or under only a few inches of water, showed as beige. The embayments in the reef, and the channels penetrating it, were blue-green and labyrinthine. The binoculars swung past the standing boy, and I realized, too late, that I had seen him. I backtracked jerkily but failed to find him again. I had to raise my eyes from the eyepieces, locate the dot of the boy again, and point the binoculars his way to bring him into focus.

The reef flat was so vast, in relation to a human, that to a passing glance it might have seemed deserted. In fact it was busy, but busy at very wide intervals. A mile beyond the boys, at the edge of the blue-green water marking the reef drop-off, were several men with casting nets. I watched them for a while, then lowered my binoculars toward the dot of a human closer to land.

This proved to be a woman. She was a big woman, barebreasted, her hair done up in a bun. She was collecting dark, foot-long objects from the shallow bottom and stuffing them in her basket. From time to time she would stop, squat, take one of the long objects, cut it, do something quick and intricate, then throw the pieces of the object back into the water. Squatting still, she would take a green bottle from her basket, unreel some invisible line from it, then reel the line back in again. I would have been mystified, except that I had seen this ritual before. The objects were sea cucumbers – sea slugs, holothurians. She was cutting them open, removing the intestines for bait, and throwing the rest away. The discarded parts were not wasted, I knew. The larger half of each sea cucumber would regenerate a whole new animal – or so I had been told by Micronesians. If the sea cucumber was divided carefully down the middle, each half would regenerate. The woman, then, was sowing the reef flat with the dragon's teeth of holothurian fragments.

Shifting my attention from the woman, I began traveling telescopically around the reef. As I played about, a thought occurred.

By swinging the binoculars through a quarter of their vertical arc, I realized, I was making a transect of the entire world of the Ponapean – the world of any Micronesian. Directly below the rail was the dark-green of coconut palms, the lighter green of banana trees, the still lighter green of dryland taro – all of them tints of the Micronesian diet. Aiming the binoculars downward, point-blank at the vegetation, I could have counted the aphids on the taro leaves, if I had been interested in counting aphids. Tilting the glasses up, I passed first the fringing reef, which provided Micronesians with protein in the varied and varicolored forms of sea cucumbers, clams, octopi, and small fishes; then passed the blue-green lagoonal water of intermediate depths, which Micronesians fished a bit and traveled as roads between coastal villages; then passed the scallop-edged, surf-whitened barrier reef, which sheltered their inside waters and provided more clams, sea cucumbers, and octopi; and arrived finally at the dark-blue of the Pacific, which they fished for tuna and turtles and sharks and on which they traveled, the great, curbless highway of it, to other islands.

When I found the woman again, she was striding south. Her stride was stately, as strides tend to be in men and women who walk a lot through shallow water. She had powerful arms and shoulders. Her breasts were huge, heroic, in keeping with the larger-than-life world on the far side of the binoculars.

My entire attention was on that sunlit world. It was funny how badly I wanted, suddenly, to be out in it. The shadow world of the hotel bar was slipping away fast, losing even that gray two-dimensionality it still possessed for me. Its only reminder was an occasional crackling from an electric insect-killer that hung high and to my left.

The insect-killer worked like this: On top was a 'black' light, a tiny blue-violet moon to which insects were attracted even in daytime. Flying to the light, they hit a grid of wires and electrocuted themselves. With a brief crackle, the spirit of each bug announced its departure from this universe.

I gave the shadow world of the bar a last, passing thought. I remembered those 19th-century Europeans who, huddled over gins in their dim taverns, imagined the land of the lotus-eaters to be somewhere in the South Pacific. How peculiar. The land of the lotus-eaters was their own. The land of wakefulness was out here.

Down on the reef flat, a young Ponapean man with a casting net over his shoulder was striding toward the heroic woman. The man wore a canvas tennis hat covered with camouflage patterns in olive and brown. He slip-dragged his feet forward in the way of net-fishermen, a step slow and dignified, intended to disturb the water minimally and not frighten the fish. At the moment he was walking that way from habit, mostly, for he hardly looked at the water; he was headed, clearly, for a rendezvous with the woman.

Twenty feet from her, he stopped. They conversed. I could not tell from the way they stood whether they were man and wife, brother and sister, mother and son. Maybe they were just acquaintances. The conversation languished, and the woman, looking off, absently hiked up her lava-lava to cover her breasts. As they prepared to part ways, the woman took several fish from her basket. Silvery, they flashed in the sun as she tossed them toward the man. The fish made a last, passive swim on their sides along the surface. When they had crossed the luminous interval between the fisherman and fisherwoman, he retrieved them, one by one.

I might have taken up residence forever in the binoculars, had I not felt a shadow presence materialize in the shadow world behind. The presence was making a quiet demand. I ignored it for a moment; then the awareness developed, like a piece of film, that a young girl from the terrace table had come up and was waiting for her turn at the binoculars. The bright world of the reef receded. I left my place at the rail and returned to my stool.

I took a sip of lethal blue from the beaded glass.

It could be, of course, that my infatuation with the reef was compounded mostly of gin and the magic enlargement of the binoculars. My division of Creation into the world of the reef and the world of the bar may seem a little too neat or drastic. Strange, but I don't believe it is. The world of the bar truly is a false world, in my estimation; false at least in Micronesia, where its introduction has been so recent. If there is a bias in what follows, it is that Micronesians should look less to the models of the West; less to credit cards, fossil fuels, tourist money, bars. They should tend to their small pieces of land, to the reef and ocean that have sustained them through the millennia they've spent here becoming who they are.

Betel nut for sale, Yap Airport, Yap,
Federated States of Micronesia.

Outer island mother and child, Yap Airport, Yap,
Federated States of Micronesia.

# A sea of small islands

The 2,105 islands and countless islets of Micronesia are scattered across three million square miles of the equatorial Pacific. 'Micronesia' derives from the Greek *mikros*, 'small,' and *nesos*, 'island.' It's a good name; the region's islands are small indeed. The combined landmass of Micronesia, if 'mass' is the right word, is hardly 1,000 square miles. Thus in a watery realm the size of the contiguous United States, dry earth amounts to one-twentieth the area of Rhode Island. There is less terra firma here than in Polynesia, the 'many islands' that lie to the southeast, or in Melanesia, the 'black islands' of dark-skinned people to the south, or in Indonesia, the 'Indian islands' to the southwest. Nowhere in the Pacific do islanders have so little underfoot. Nowhere are they thrown back so irrevocably on the resources of the sea.

There are two kinds of landform in Micronesia, 'high' islands and 'low.' The high islands are volcanic, often large, sometimes steep – a few rise several thousand feet – and usually jungle-covered, though the northernmost reach into a drier belt of the Pacific, have undergone more recent vulcanism, and remain relatively bare. The low islands are made of coral. They are crowns of living and once-living material perched atop submerged volcanoes. They come as atolls – rings of coral islets encircling a lagoon – or as semi-atolls, or as solitaries. Some are as low as six feet above sea level. Few have altitudes of over 30 feet.

Micronesia is divided into four archipelagos.

Easternmost are the Marshalls, a chain, or double chain, composed entirely of coral atolls. One of these atolls, Kwajalein, is 80 miles long and encloses a lagoon of 840 square miles – the largest atoll in the world. Most Marshallese atolls remain what they should be, places few people ever heard of: Mili, Ujae, Wotho, Lae, Ebon, Arno, Namu, Majuro, Likiep, Jaluit, Namoruk, Utirik, Maloelap, Ailinglaplap, and so on. Two, through a fate no atoll or island people ever deserved, became world famous: Rongelap and Bikini.

Beginning in the center of Micronesia and running to its western edge are the Caroline Islands, the longest and most diverse of Micronesia's archipelagos. The Carolines are composed both of high and low islands. The Carolines' high islands, or high-island clusters, are Kosrae, Ponape, Truk, Yap, and Palau. These are the Carolinian names vaguely familiar to the outside world, if a Carolinian name is to ring any bell at all. They are reasonably big islands. They have, to my ear at least, big-sounding names. The low islands of the Carolines are small places with small-sounding names: Eo, Aga, Ant, Asor, Eau, Elin, Edat, Etal, Elato, Eauripik, Otta, Oman, Ozen, Igup-I, Ifaluk, Ulul, Utagal, Onanet, Fais, Foro, Fananan, Fanamar, Fanuet, Fanuela, Falauaw, Faleu, Falaite, Falifi, Falasit, Falalais, Falalep, Falalop, Faraulep, Fanadik, Feinif, Fourup, Pau, Pig, Pugue, Pikelot, Pigaras, Pulap, Punlop, Puluwab, Puluwat, Pulusuk, Nama, Namoluk, Ngulu, Mor, Moch, Mokil, Mogmog, Merir, Raur, Losap, Losiep, Lamotrek, Sorol, Sonsorol, Sing, Siliap, Siteng, Satawan, Satawal, Taki, Tobi, Gielap.

Northernmost in Micronesia are the Marianas. The islands of this chain are composed entirely of volcanic rock and upraised coral limestone. Guam, the southernmost of the Marianas, is the largest island in all Micronesia. Guam's interior jungle is dense enough for the second-to-the-last straggler from the Japanese Imperial Army to have hidden out in it from the Americans until 1972. North of Guam is the island of Rota, where the last of the free Natives hid out from the Spanish after the Jesuits and soldiers had forced the evacuation of all the other northern Marianas. North of Rota is Tinian, the island from which, 250 years after the Spanish evacuation and 27 years before the surrender of the Japanese straggler, the *Enola Gay* took off for Hiroshima with her special bombload. North of Tinian is Saipan, a famous island battleground in the war that the flight of *Enola Gay* ended. North of Saipan, the slight north-by-northwestern arc of the archipelago curves into obscurity. The island names are, once more, names that the outside world has somehow missed entirely: Farallon de Medinilla, Anatahan, Sarigan, Guguan, Alamagan.

The fourth, last, and southeasternmost of Micronesia's groups is the Gilberts. The Gilberts are coral atolls. They are the only Micronesian group to lie partly south of the equator. Geographically part of Micronesia, they are politically separate. Neither they, nor the solitary Micronesian islands of Nauru and Banaba, were entrusted to the United States to be administered by the United States Trust Territory of the Pacific Islands after the war. For this reason, the Gilberts are often excluded from discussions of Micronesia. It is an oversight that does not hurt Gilbertese feelings unduly; 'Micronesia' is a doubtful entity to begin with, a convenience for First World geographers that has never proved all that convenient, its boundaries not coincident with those of any of the old empires in this part of the ocean, its unity unrecognized by Gilbertese tradition or the traditions of any other Micronesian people.

Micronesia's climate is tropical maritime. The onerous, egg-fry-on-the-pavement heat of equatorial regions on the continents is moderated here by the influence of the ocean. Temperatures average in the eighties. Humidity is high. Rainfall varies. The high, green islands of Ponape and Kosrae receive 180 inches a year, but the northern Marianas and the northern Marshalls, lying beyond the margins of the equatorial wet belt, receive just 70 to 80 inches. Percolating into the volcanic soils of the northernmost Marianas, those 70 to 80 inches disappear quickly. Their disappearance works no hardship on people, since those northernmost islands are uninhabited. Percolating into the sandy soils of the inhabited northern Marshalls, the 70 to 80 inches disappear quickly too, and the Marshallese people suffer periodic droughts. The Marshallese do not, however, suffer typhoons. Caroline Islanders do, and with a vengeance. In the Carolines and the Marianas, people never go thirsty, but they sometimes lose their roofs to 200-mile-per-hour winds.

The terrestrial ecosystems of Micronesia's islands vary greatly in complexity. The larger the islands are, and the closer they lie to big landmasses, the more diverse their floras and faunas. The Palaus, a group of large islands just 500 miles north of the mini-continent of New Guinea – an enormous island which, in its turn, is close to the real continents of Asia and Australia – are islands nearly continental in their biological diversity. The ocean has proved to be this planet's most effective barrier to the spread of species, and Palau, Yap, and the Marianas don't lie in the middle of a lot of ocean. In remoter corners of the Carolines and the

13

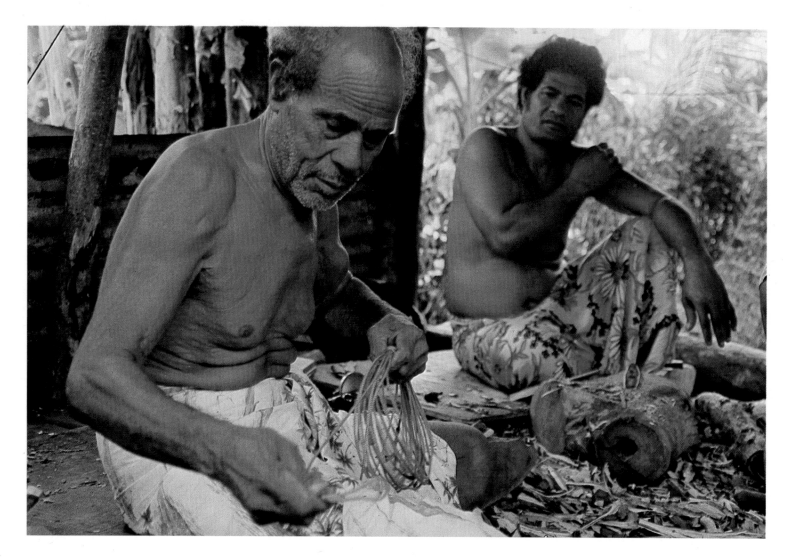

Craftsmen, Kapingamarangi enclave, Ponape,
Federated States of Micronesia.

Yapese man in *thu*, at Colonia town, Yap,
Federated States of Micronesia.

Marshalls, however, nearly lost in endless blue, are tiny coral islands nearly as simple, ecologically, as those islands in magazine cartoons – a heap of sand and a single coconut palm. Few plant and animal migrants find these places; and fewer still, having found them, find the means – the soil, shade, water – that allow them to stay.

The marine ecosystems of small and remote islands tend to be simpler, too, but there the disparity is not so enormous. The ocean is less a barrier to sea creatures than it is to land creatures, obviously. It remains more a barrier than one might think. For inhabitants of the shallow benthos – the bottom dwellers who build and inhabit the reef – the deep water of the open ocean is a wasteland difficult to cross. Yet adult reef fish, their planktonic larvae, and the planktonic larvae of corals and other invertebrate reef dwellers, do manage to swim, or drift, to the smallest of islands. Above water, that cartoon island of sand and a single coconut palm may look like the work of an infant Creator just starting out, but underwater it is as diverse as anything under this sun.

Islands large enough to possess what can be called interiors are covered by mixed-species forests and savannahs inhabited by centipedes, millipedes, scorpions, termites, hermit crabs, land crabs, coconut crabs, frogs, geckoes, monitor lizards, tree snakes, blind burrowing snakes, boa constrictors, herons, ospreys, pigeons, plover, and parrots. In one group, the Palaus, there are crocodiles. The islands are poor in mammals. There are introduced mammal species, like rats, dogs, cats, pigs, and carabao, but other than man, who introduced himself by boat, the only native mammals are the flying kind: bats, both insect-eating and fruit-eating.

Micronesians do a little logging in their forests. On islands big enough for streams, they trap freshwater shrimp. They forage their interiors for herbs, both magic and medicinal, and for the eggs of incubator birds. They hunt their forests for pigeons and fruit bats. This inland hunting, fishing, and foraging often seems more sport than serious business. Fruit bats are the Micronesian *escargot*, pigeons the caviar. Half the fun of hunting fruit bats, half the luxury of their taste, seems to arise from the novelty of getting food from land.

The real meat on the Micronesian table – on the Micronesian floor, rather, since tables have never really caught on in the islands – comes from the reef and the blue water outside it. The real potatoes grow in taro patches, on breadfruit trees, and in yam and cassava gardens close to shore. Micronesians are a people of the shoreline. Even on high islands with roomy interiors, like Truk, Kosrae, and Ponape, the villages tend to cluster along the water. Micronesians like to have the sea breeze flapping in their clotheslines. They like the sound of the surf in their ears, the blue line of the horizon in their eyes. They like the ready access to those salty pastures of reef, and proximity to that ocean highway their ancestors traveled here.

There is no general agreement as to who, exactly, the Micronesians are and where they come from. There are aboriginal theories on the matter, but most have fallen into disfavor, even with the aborigines. The Palau Islanders, for example, once believed that they began as maggots on the corpse of Uab, the enormous demigod whose exploded parts became the islands of Palau. Few if any Palauans believe that any longer.

But Western theories, too, get worn and rusty. Few if any anthropologists believe the 'wave' or 'horde' theories held by their colleagues of 30 years ago. According to the wave theories of Oceanic settlement, hordes from Asia made orderly progress outward into the Pacific, traveling the stepping stones of island chains. Anthropologists of the present generation believe there was more ricochet and back-eddy in Pacific migrations than the wave theories allowed for. The wave theorists were hampered, too, by the notion of race then in vogue that mankind has three main branches. To Peter Buck, a prominent wave theorist of the 1930s, it seemed clear that the Micronesians had more in common with the 'Caucasoid' Polynesians than with the 'Negroid' Melanesians, which led him to the opinion that Micronesia was colonized first by Polynesians moving northward from their own islands, then by 'Mongoloid' peoples who came in afterward and muddied the racial picture.

This scheme, though probably an improvement on the maggot theory of the Palau Islanders, suffers from being too simple. Our notions about race become increasingly complex with time. Racial theories speciate, just as race itself does. A three-race scheme is not much help in unraveling Micronesia's genealogy. Anthropologists today are inclined to believe that Micronesia was settled not by pure-race hordes, but by the mixed-bag arrival of one canoe here, two canoes there, the passengers blown off course by storm or fleeing some calamity in their home islands.

If there is a consensus among scientists today, it is that the colonization of Micronesia was two-pronged.

The western islands of Palau, Yap, and the Marianas were settled first, by peoples from Indonesia and the Philippines. The primary evidence for this separate settlement of the west is linguistic. The languages of these three western groups are Austronesian (Malayo-Polynesian) languages of an Indonesian type. They have nothing in common with the rest of Micronesia.

Eastern and central Micronesia were settled later, by eastern-Austronesian-speaking people with Melanesian origins, probably in the area of Fiji and the New Hebrides. These later, eastern settlers became the experts at living on small coral islands, and it was they, in the end, who would settle the very westernmost islands of Micronesia – the small islands of Sonsorol, Tobi, Pulo Anna, and Merir, which are geographically and politically part of Palau, but linguistically and culturally part of the central Carolines.

This two-pronged theory, of course, is sure to undergo revision. Its clear lines will become fuzzy with footnotes, and in time its inventors will no longer recognize it.

I wonder myself about the notion that Palau was settled primarily from the Philippines and Indonesia. The Philippines are indeed close to Palau, but so is Melanesia. Of all Micronesia's archipelagos, Palau is nearest Melanesia, lying just 500 miles north of Papua New Guinea. The Palauan people, to my eye at least, are the most Melanesian-looking of Micronesians. Individuals with very dark skin and nappy hair seem more numerous in Palau than anywhere else in Micronesia. I suspect there are more than a few

Palauans resting after day's work, Ngeremlengui, Palau,
Republic of Belau.

Two boys, awaiting arrival of passengers at Yap Airport, Yap,
Federated States of Micronesia.

Papuans in Palau's woodpile. Melanesians were certainly capable of making the crossing to Palau. Until recent times, war canoes from New Guinea sporadically raided Palau's southwestern satellites, Sonsorol, Merir, and Tobi, just 200 miles south of the main group. There are, as well, cultural similarities between Palau and the New Guinea island of Manus that strongly suggest a former connection.

I accept the testimony of the linguists that Palauan is a language of an Indonesian type. Palauan certainly does not *sound* anything like the languages of the rest of Micronesia. To many foreign ears, mine among them, Palauan is the most dramatic of Micronesian tongues. Palauans seem to spend more time enjoying their language, punning and otherwise playing around with it, than do other islanders.

I wish to propose, then, a theory of my own, a neat scheme for time to wreck:

Palau was colonized by dark Melanesian hordes from New Guinea. They were bright people but etymologically blighted, saddled with a bland and boring mother tongue. Today, the Palau Islands, along with Ponape and Kosrae, are thought to be the loveliest in Micronesia, but those first Palauans, lacking a vocabulary adequate to express it, found a measure of that loveliness escaping them. They knew something was wrong, but they couldn't put the collective finger of their brand-new race on it. And so things continued for a millennium, until a canoeload of Indonesian poets, voyaging from their home island to a culture fest on a neighboring island, encountered a storm. They were better poets than sailors. The canoe was blown off course, to wash ashore some weeks later on one of Palau's green islands. The chief of that island, muttering darkly in his miserable native tongue, was about to light the kindling under a poet-filled cauldron, when one of the poets, composing verse at light speed under the pressure of his deadline, spoke.

It is interesting that the Micronesians themselves have no racial memories, not even doubtful ones, of the mainland from which they came.

The Tobi Islanders recollect origins in the Micronesian atoll of

Ulithi to the north. The people of Ponape tell tales of their own origins in Kosrae to the south. The people of Kayangel Atoll believe they are descended from a tyrannical race who once ruled Ngeruangel, the abandoned, typhoon-ruined semi-atoll northwest of them. But none of these recollections goes beyond the Pacific's screen of islands. Not one of Micronesia's oral histories makes reference to a great landmass of origin. The Micronesians have been sea people, island-dwellers, for so long that, prior to their contact with Europeans, the *idea* of continents was lost to them.

Micronesians are a heterogeneous people of medium stature, high cheekbones, straight to wavy to frizzy hair, and complexions that range from *café au lait* through various chocolates to nearly black. The islands have always been a mixing ground, and their inhabitants are too diverse to be really considered a people. Two islands of the geographer's Micronesia, Nukuoro and Kapingamarangi, do not belong at all in the anthropologist's Micronesia. Both are inhabited by Polynesian-speaking people of Polynesian physical type and culture. The other islands of Micronesia have, in varying degrees and particulars, affinities with all the outlying 'nesias. They owe this word to Indonesia, that kinship system to Melanesia, this supra-occipital arch to Polynesia. And in turn those three southerly 'nesias owe certain things to Micronesia. The Fijians of Melanesia, for example, owe to the Carolinians certain refinements in outrigger-canoe design.

Much of this mixing was prehistoric, but it has continued into historic times. Today the Chamorros, the natives of the Marianas, no longer resemble the Chamorros who inhabited those islands in 1521, when Ferdinand Magellan discovered them. Having experienced the longest and most intense contact with the outside world, the Marianas people comprise a new race of mixed Chamorro, Spanish, Filipino, Portuguese, and Mexican ancestry.

In this century, Germany ruled Micronesia for 14 years, Japan for 30, the United States for 35. A few colonial administrators have been lecherous, many just human, and today many Micronesians have Japanese and American blood.

Micronesians speak nine, or 12, or 14 major languages, depending on how fine a linguist wants to draw his distinctions.

Micronesian kinship systems are varied and, to a Westerner, confusing. Anthropologist Leonard Mason explains the system in operation on Yap, Ulithi, Truk, Ponape, and the Mortlock Islands thus: *This is the 'Crow' type, in which relatives in a female line of descent are emphasized and generation is ignored. In cousin terminology, the speaker refers to his father's sister's children as 'mother' and 'father' and, reciprocally, applies the term 'child' to his mother's brother's children. His other cousins are classed as siblings.*

The system practiced in the Marshalls and on Nauru is the 'Iroquois' type. In those islands, according to Mason, *special terms exist for mother's brother and sister's son, but also a difference appears in the cousin terminology. Children of father's brother and mother's sister are regarded as siblings; and, where the opposite sex is involved, this relationship carries the same restraint and sexual avoidance as for real siblings.*

Rank in some islands is inherited matrilineally, in others patrilineally. Land is the rarest of commodities in Micronesia, and its ownership is at the heart of Micronesia's lineage and ranking systems. It is nearly impossible to alienate land in the islands, as numerous foreign administrators have found out. Land is owned by lineage, clan, or municipality and it is difficult to get it away from them. Tools, in the old days, were made of stone, coral, shell, and wood. Fabric was of pandanus, hibiscus, or coconut fiber. Today steel and aluminum and factory-woven cloth have largely replaced those materials on all but the most remote of outer islands.

There are myths about Micronesia, as about Oceania generally, that can't be bludgeoned to death. Nice myths, they have a way of propagating themselves. David Nevin's recent *The American Touch in Micronesia*, while correct in most of its basic arguments, is mythological in many of its asides. *The coconut palm grows wherever the sea hurls its nuts*, Nevin writes, and, *man is in harmony and the living is easy.* Coconut palms grow, in fact, wherever Micronesians bust their own nuts to plant them. A few coconut trees do take root on the strand where the high tide deposits them, and it is easy to see how a brief visitor, looking down from the treeline to the ingenious, salt-resistant, survival package/dispersal mechanism of a coconut bobbing offshore, could assume that all the trees had

Brittle star, Majuro reef,
Marshall Islands.

Lagoon beach, Majuro,
Marshall Islands.

begun that way. The unidyllic truth is that the palm forests of inhabited islands are plantations, begun from seedlings and maintained by the sweat of Micronesian brows.

The most annoying and persistent of the myths about Pacific Islands is that 'the living is easy.' David Nevin, and anyone else under that illusion, should try climbing one of those coconut palms. He and they should spend a day of stoop labor with the women in the taro swamp – the hardest work in Micronesia – and should emerge mud-covered with those matrons and girls in the twilight. He should spend a day under the tropical sun with a spearfisherman on the reef. The only easy Micronesian living, I submit, is at the typewriters of folk like me and David Nevin.

It is tempting to assume, given the small size of the islands and a material culture which, until recently, was all wood, shell, and stone, that Micronesians are a simple people. The tendency of almost all Western descriptions is to simplify Micronesians and their lives.

A pernicious thing about the myth that the subsistence life is easy or simple is a corollary assumption: that subsistence skills, once lost, will be easy to recover. If all else fails, it is often argued, Micronesians can always go back to being subsistence farmers and fishermen. The truth is that subsistence skills are more difficult to learn than those of technological society.

That possibility first dawned on me, I think, 10 years ago, as I idly watched a Micronesian boy throwing a fish spear at Coke cans alongside the road. I hardly paid attention until I realized that the boy never missed.

The Micronesian apprentice navigator spends years memorizing hundreds of star courses between islands. He learns long lists of sea marks – underwater reefs, and so forth – and of sea animals he can expect to see between the various pairs of islands in his system. He learns the ranges of various sea birds and how to interpret bird behavior. His only chronometer is inside his head. He must develop and refine that biological timepiece until it, and his sea sense, can accurately measure current set, gale set, and wind drift. With his internal clock, in conjuction with an ingenious system of 'reference' islands, he divides his voyage into segments, thereby keeping track of the distance he has covered. Tacking, he uses a similar system to divide into segments the distance covered on each tack, mentally following the progress of his destination island – following its *position*, since the island itself is invisible to him – as it moves under certain reference stars along the horizon. He must be immune to fatigue. He almost never sleeps, even on voyages of many days and many hundreds of miles, for his is a dead-reckoning system of navigation, and he must keep a running log of the voyage in his head.

A casual observer, looking down on the canoe from the high rail of some titanic cruise ship and seeing the barefoot, tattooed man sitting crosslegged on the small and apparently rude vessel below, might be excused for mistaking the navigator for something less intricate than what he is: a computer in a loincloth.

In the Carolines, the instruction periods for serious navigators sometimes last six months or a year. During that time, the student and his classmates are confined to the men's clubhouse of their island. They see no women. The only males they see, besides their teachers, are the men who bring them food. They study from the moment they rise to the moment they sleep.

In the West, law students like to think they suffer in preparing for bar exams. Ph.D. candidates like to moan about their orals. They should, for perspective, wake on a hard plank floor in a men's house to which they have been confined for months, without women, and look into the beady eyes of the tattooed old instructor whose shift this is, and who has been waiting, patiently, for the eyes to come open so his lecture can resume.

Fishermen in Micronesia bear only the flimsiest of resemblances to Western weekend warriors wearing waders and hats bristly with tied flies. The coral reef is a system infinitely more complex than a trout stream. It is vastly more complex than the pelagic ecosystem fished by commercial tuna boats. In some inshore waters of Micronesia, marine biologists estimate, as much as half of the biota are species unknown to science. Learning to fish such a system takes a lifetime. The knowledge of fish possessed by old Micronesian fishermen – of fish habits, seasons, cycles, locations – is encyclopaedic. The variety and ingenuity of fishing techniques practiced in Micronesia is staggering. None of it comes simply or easily. It is acquired through years of observation and honed by the necessities of putting food on the table and maintaining prestige in a community of sea people.

Many Micronesians are no longer sea people, of course. The subsistence life is moribund or dead in parts of the islands. Today Micronesians are cab drivers, priests, high-school teachers, cops, truck drivers, masons, electricians, businessmen. This Westernized employment is confined mostly to the administrative centers. Around the edges of the town live men and women who practice something very close to the traditional life. A few miles from the downtown streets of Palau's capital, there are men who still hunt pigeons with blowguns in the forest. On Ponape there is a hotel bar from which you can still watch boy fishermen and women holothurian hunters on the reef.

It is probably good that these things endure. The 'West' of Micronesia's dusty streets is an imitation West, a false façade maintained artificially by money pumped in from the outside. Façades like that sometimes fall.

Modern Micronesians have demonstrated no special, serendipitous knack for anything about the technological world. They have not manifested the Iroquois' gift for high construction work, nor the Ghurkas' for modern warfare. They don't, like the Eskimos, have an uncanny way with machines. The Marshall Islands do seem to be producing 20th-century leaders much faster than one would expect in islands so remote and so recently emerged from the Shell Age. Palauans have shown an aptitude for business. But the Micronesian genius, gift, and talent, the thing the islanders are uncanny at, the art and the science in which no other people surpass them, is their alliance with the sea.

Rock Islands, Palau,
Republic of Belau.

Bamboo raft, Koror-Babeldaob channel, Palau,
Republic of Belau.

# Canoes

The greatest ocean on earth was discovered, explored, and settled by canoe. No one knows how the first fleets of this great enterprise looked. Constructed of wood, palm leaves, sennit, and tree sap, the earliest Pacific canoes have long since returned to the elements. The only blueprints that ever existed for them were locked in the brains of the builders, Paleolithic men who themselves reverted to dust thousands of years before Christ. We do know, however, what the voyaging canoes of the latter stages of Pacific exploration looked like. Fifteen hundred years after Christ, men with notebooks and long-quilled pens descried and described them. They were of two principal kinds: the double-hulled canoes of Polynesia, and the outrigger canoes of Micronesia. In Fiji, the two designs came together in the canoe the Fijians called *ndrua*, which had double hulls, as in Polynesia, but with one hull shorter than the other, on the principle of the Micronesian outrigger float. It was the first two designs, though, that logged the most millions of nautical miles and discovered the most land.

If 'canoe' suggests a small vessel of birch bark or animal skin on still waters, then the word is misleading. Polynesian and Micronesian canoes were *ships* longer and faster than the first European vessels to come among them. The canoes of Oceania were sometimes more than 100 feet long, could carry more than 200 men, and sailed seas that can blow the wildest on earth. The Polynesian canoe, with its bigger capacity for passengers and freight, was the better canoe for long voyages. The Micronesian was faster and more maneuverable. Polynesian sailors were the greater explorers and adventurers. Their bold, cross-hemispheric voyages to Hawaii were epics without parallel in Oceanic history. But Polynesians were not the best navigators. The traits for fearless adventurer and good navigator may even be incompatible. The spirit that sent the Polynesian captain full of faith across thousands of miles of empty ocean is not the cautious, conservative spirit of the accurate land-finder. Discovering Hawaii was a feat of seamanship, not of navigation. The Polynesian captain was just *going*, he didn't know where. Finding his way back to Polynesia with the news of his find required some navigational skills, but not a lot, in that the islands of Polynesia make a relatively dense cluster and accordingly are hard to miss.

The best navigators in all Oceania were the Micronesians, whose small islands were spread out and hard to find.

Navigational science is not evenly distributed in Micronesia. The best navigators come from the smallest islands. The greatest Micronesian travelers, of necessity, have been the inhabitants of little coral islands poor in one resource or another. For tobacco, or for sea turtles, or just to see new faces, the small-islanders throughout history have had to jump in their canoes and set off.

The Micronesian languages with the widest geographic distribution are those of the Marshalls and the central Carolines, archipelagos of small islands. There was always constant human interchange between those specks of coral. In a curious way, the smaller and remoter islands of Micronesia were the least isolated.

The Micronesian languages with the most restricted distribution were those of the volcanic islands. Those 'high' islands were self-contained worlds, fertile inland, skirted by rich reefs, big enough to divide into minor nations or states, with plenty of new faces in villages on the other side of the hill. Sailors from the big islands trolled and bottom-fished just outside their reefs, but needed to go no farther. In a curious way, the high-islanders, though they received deference and tribute from the low-islanders of the coral atolls outlying them, were more provincial than their subjects.

There were exceptions. The high-islanders of Yap, for example, were, until recent times, in the habit of voyaging across open ocean to Palau to quarry the great stones they use for money. And the low-islanders of Puluwat, who are perhaps the best navigators of the central Carolines, have never played self-effacing countrymen. The Puluwatans were as skillful at piracy as they were at navigation. They bullied their low-island neighbors and sometimes even raided the Truk Lagoon, the high islands in the middle of which, at least in the estimation of geographers, make the center to which Puluwat is satellite. Most Micronesian islands have their home-grown form of self-defense techniques, and the Puluwatan style is regarded as especially potent.

But in general the law holds true. Small land, big seamen; and the reverse. The Micronesians who inhabit high islands were probably once master navigators, but the talent has atrophied. Men come to high volcanic islands much as corals do. The coral larvae row in on hairlike oars, attach themselves to the volcanic substrate, and become polyps, building castles of calcium carbonate and shedding those hair-like oars. Men sail in, erect their house stones of calcium carbonate, their cities of basalt, and they reef their sails.

By the time Europeans arrived at Kosrae, the inhabitants of that high island had ceased to be open-ocean sailors. The most impressive canoes found by Frederic Lütke, who visited the island in 1824, were not sailing vessels, but what Lütke called *pirogues de parade*, the paddling canoes of the king. *They never go outside the reefs,* Lütke wrote. *Having no occasion for voyaging, they make no use of sails.*

The Kosraean pirogues were dugouts 25 to 30 feet long and they carried eight to 10 paddlers. The hulls, painted with red ocher and then polished, were light and they drew little water. The lashing that joined the outrigger float to the outrigger boom was complex and lovely; formed of different colored strands of sennit, it made a diamond pattern.

James Hornell, in *Canoes of Oceania*, the 1936 classic that remains the last word on the subject of Pacific canoes, writes, *This system of connecting the float to the boom is the most intricate with which I am acquainted, and bespeaks a long experience in the construction of outriggers, coupled with intelligence and invention of a high order. The conclusion is forced upon the observer that these canoes must have had ancestors of great size and rigged with at least equal skill to that shown by their immediate neighbors, both east and west.*

A century and a half after Lütke – 44 years after Hornell – I spoke on Kosrae with Nena William, perhaps the best Kosraean canoe-maker of the present day. His countrymen had chosen William to demonstrate canoe-carrying at the South Pacific Festival of Arts, to be held in New Guinea. Yet Nena William did not seem at all impressed with himself. By his manner, he seemed to agree with James Hornell that marine design in Kosrae is in a devolutionary period. He seemed puzzled that I was interested in Kosrae's canoes, and not, say, in Kosraean limes.

War canoe, *Kesebekuu* (Moray eel) of Airai, Palau,
Republic of Belau.

Young Palauan asleep on top of war canoe *Kesebekuu* (Moray eel) in Airai canoe house, Palau, Republic of Belau.

*Before, there were so many people who could build canoes,* he said. *Now there are few. I learned from my own father. I used to work alongside him when he was building a canoe. The kind of canoe I'm building now is not hard. There was another kind, though, built for racing. Not anybody could build it. Not just anybody could touch it. The specifications were very fine.*

The canoe under construction rested in the shade of a thatch shelter at the top of the beach, on a bed of chips from its mother log. The canoe had borrowed its basic shape from the log; its sides were rounded, wider at the turn of the bilge than at the gunwale. Beside the canoe-in-progress was a completed canoe, newly painted white with a yellow trim. I had seen similar paddling canoes resting everywhere in Kosrae. They sat beside Kosrae's thatch or plank houses like cars in driveways, or in the shade of trees above the beach, uncovered sometimes, and sometimes protected by mats against the wood-cracking heat of the sun. I had seen them, too, with paddlers in their sterns, their prows slicing the still lagoon waters, their wakes first dividing, then fracturing and jumbling, the inverted jungle mountain reflected greenly there. On most other high islands of Micronesia, speedboats with outboard engines now outnumber paddling canoes, but on Kosrae, there are few outboards to be seen, and most small commerce is still in dugouts. The age of voyaging canoes may be over in Kosrae, but the age of canoes is not.

Nena William sat in a circle of his friends, taking a break. He and several of the others had received haircuts moments before I arrived. The style was radical bowl-cut — very close on the sides, tall on top. The men, like the canoe, were surrounded by shavings. The canoe's chips were blond, the men's black. William's arms were strong, his eyes amused and intelligent.

*First we look at the tree itself,* he said. *See how well it's structured, see that it's straight. Not everybody building canoes nowadays knows how to select a proper tree. We have to go up to the mountain.*

*When the tree is still standing, we can tell which side will be up and down — which side will be the top of the canoe, which one the bottom. We can decide that better when the tree is still standing. Then we cut it down.*

*We rough it, where it lies, into the shape of the canoe. Then we haul it down the mountain. Each time we yank, we sing a song. This will give moral support and power for the pulling. We sing with heavy work of any kind. Whoever leads the song must be knowledgeable about that song, otherwise it will be very heavy to drag that whole thing.*

*When we get it down, we start digging out the dugout. The length depends on who's buying it and what he wants. A canoe six or seven feet long would take one man a week. Three or four men would take two or three days. The sides are a half-inch thick. While we carve, we hit the sides with our hands to gauge the thickness.*

And that, according to Nena William, was all there was to it. I knew for certain, though, that I was losing a lot in translation. The English answers to my questions were much too brief to be faithful to the long debates in Kosraean that preceded them.

*What kind of tree do you use?* I asked, for example.

For five minutes, the Kosraeans argued and gestured and laughed. Canoes were not a dead issue here, obviously; the great age of Kosraean seamanship might be over, but plenty of feeling for canoes remained. The discussion finally petered out, and the Kosraeans remembered me. *Elak*, Nena William answered.

\* \* \*

The Palaus are another group of high islands where voyaging had ceased by the time of contact with Europeans.

Of all Micronesian groups, Palau is nearest to being a complete world in itself. There was no need to sail off in search of another. Palau's reef is the most extensive, diverse, and productive in Micronesia. The volcanoes that formed most of Babeldaob, Koror, and Ngarakabesang, the three close-clustered islands where most Palauans live and lived, were old, worn volcanoes that made a rolling landscape easy to farm.

The natives of Yap to the north had to sail to Palau to quarry the massive stone disks they use for money, but the Palauans required nothing like that of Yap. Palauan money was, and is, in the form of glass and ceramic beads and bars of mysterious origin. Some of it may have come from Indonesia, where glass beads are known to have existed in prehistoric times, but no one knows for sure. Palauans must once have been aware of its place of origin, but for centuries that knowledge has been lost, and it made no sense to sail in search of more, in the absence of some notion as to which way to head. Besides, why ruin a good thing? Palauan money is impossible to counterfeit, partly for technical reasons but mostly because every piece is catalogued in the minds of elder Palauans: whether its shape is round or oval or cylindrical or faceted; whether it is a yellow bar of fired clay called *bachel berrak* or *bleob berrak*, or of the red bars of fired clay called *bachel mungungau* and *bleob mungungau*, or of the dark glass beads called *chelbucheb* and *kluk* and *dlobech*, or of the clear-green glass beads called *bachel cheldoioch* and *bleob cheldoioch*. Palau's currency can only be deflationary. The beads and bars can no longer be manufactured; they can only be lost.

The Palauans exacted tribute from their Southwestern satellites, the small coral islands of Tobi, Sonsorol, Pulo Anna, and Merir, and this must have required sailing south occasionally to apply a little muscle, but Palau's system of tribute was never so elaborate or far-reaching as that of the Yap Empire.

Palauans did not even have to sail away to look for enemies. Palauan society was, and is, so thoroughly factionalized that there were plenty of enemies at home. Palau's great northern federation was continually at war with its southern federation, and within those two federations, the different states always fought, and within those states, villages squabbled, and within those villages, clans and families tussled and competed.

At the turn of the century, there were still sailing canoes in Palau, and today there are Palauans who remember them. Charles Gibbons, the *Reuer*, or fourth-ranking chief, of the central island of Koror, is an 86-year-old who has become a sort of Grandpa Moses of Palau since he turned to painting 15 years ago. The sailing canoes of his youth show up often in his paintings.

Fish carving in canoe, Ponape,
Federated States of Micronesia.

Paddling canoe prow in Moen, Truk.
Federated States of Micronesia.

Part of the appeal of Gibbons's art is in the trouble he has with tricks like perspective, and his sailing canoes often cut across the ocean at strange angles. But in their detail and proportion, Gibbons's watercolor canoes are true. His renderings of the *kaep*, the sailing canoe in which Palauans raced and fished, could have been drawn from the model in the Cologne Museum. The old artist either has a remarkable memory, or he *did* draw from the model in the Cologne Museum – or maybe sneaked a peek at some yellowing plate in a book in order to refresh his recollection. (Gibbons is in the odd position of being nearly as old as ethnology in his native islands.) The sails of Gibbons's *kaeps* are very white and gay, and his sailors always seem to be having a good time.

The average *kaep* was 33 feet long, yet had a beam of only 14 inches. In cross section, the hull was wedge shaped, with a knife-edged keel. Longitudinally, the curve of the keel was subcrescentic; the canoe bowed up so sharply at either end that the whole fore part of the vessel rode out of the water, and a good part of the stern. This convexity of the keel line was the most pronounced in Micronesia, the curve inspired, legend said, by the claw of the fruit bat. Under sail, the crewmen moved aft, which brought the canoe's head high out of the water. This reduced the underwater surface area of the hull and reduced friction; the canoe *got off*.

The *kaep's* sail was more typical of the rest of Micronesia. It was an Oceanic lateen rig, a large triangle woven of pandanus, stepped with apex downward, beautiful against a horizon. Palau was an archipelago of specialists, and sail-making was an art separate from the rest of *kaep*-making.

When the wind failed, the *kaep* became a paddling canoe. It had six thwart bars, which, in a calm, served as seats for paddlers. On the windward, or outrigger, side, the thwart bars protruded as posts, a distance equal to half again the width of the hull. At their distal ends, all six of the bars curved up slightly, and Palauan fishermen rested their spears and fishing rods there. At the end of every thwart-post, on a short length of sennit, hung a white cowry, and cowries dangled from the bow and stern. The first and last thwart-posts – or the first and first, since in Micronesian outrigger canoes either end can be the bow, the configuration of both being identical, stern becoming bow each time the canoe changes tack – were carved in the shape of the *tengadidik*, or kingfisher.

The kingfisher was there for good luck. The bird was supposed to be the sidekick of Koreomel, a sea spirit. Its perching on the mast of the spirit's canoe, whenever that magic vessel neared Palau, informed the spirit that land was close. The Palauans may have valued the kingfisher for its own spirit, as well. Palauans say, of a restless person, *Like the kingfisher, chattering while taking to wing*. To the first thwart-carver of kingfishers, perhaps, the kingfisher's ebullience seemed appropriate to a canoe spanking off under sail.

James Hornell, the Boswell and Herodotus of Pacific canoes, an expert who had seen hundreds of them, was especially smitten by the *kaep*.

*Apart from the 'tangadik' figures and egg cowries hung by short cords from the thwart bars and various parts of the outrigger*, he wrote, *the good taste of the islanders was shown by the all but total lack of extraneous ornament upon the beautifully modeled hull*. The only exception was, in some canoes, *the inlay in pearl shell of three small crosses or three circular discs on the lower and larger of the two rectangular projections from the cutwater*.

Hornell's spelling, '*tangadik*,' was wrong – he missed a syllable of the bird's call – but about the shell inlay he was correct. Charles Gibbons, the old painter, noticed those crosses of pearl shell too, and they appear in many of his watercolor sailing canoes.

*Fine as are the sailing canoes of the Caroline Islands*, continued Hornell, *none attain the slim elegance and beauty of line of this canoe, built as it was for speed. The 'kaep' was the Oceanic equivalent of the large racing cutter of Europe and America: it had no cargo capacity and was used mainly by the chiefs for display and in particular for long-distance races, exceedingly popular with these islanders.*

In the old days, a big *kaep* race was held every year in Palau. It began in Airai, the southernmost district of the big island of Babeldaob. Airai was chosen because it was the home of Medechibelau, 'He-who-grasps-Palau,' the god who, among other accomplishments, invented sailing.

From Airai, the *kaep* fleet raced the 25 miles up the west coast of Babeldaob Island, passing the nearly hidden entrance to the big, mangrove-lined bay of Ngatpang; passing, one after another, the jungly hummocks of Babeldaob's ancient volcano, the green summits worn down like old teeth, none higher than 700 feet; passing, at long intervals in the wild coast, the shoreline cluster of palms and the coral-riprap jetty that marked each village; passing finally the northern tip of Babeldaob and leaving land behind.

The prows of the canoes pointed now at an empty horizon; rather, since they rode so high, they pointed at the sky above an empty horizon. The white cowry dangling from each prow swung like a pendulum in the clouds. The racers crossed above the great underwater banks of Kossol Reef, the ocean's color changing continually under the speeding hulls, from deep blue to aquamarine to green to almost yellow, depending on the varying depths of the coral plateau beneath.

Squalls blew in. The sky darkened, the ocean went gray. The rain hit suddenly with a sibilant roar, flattening the sea and stinging the skin and the eyes of the sailors. Then the dark and ragged lower edge of the squall passed, the sun came out, the sea turned blue, and the waves scintillated.

The horizon was not empty long. Soon the islands of Kayangel Atoll appeared there, four green rafts on the ocean, only the tops of the palms visible at first over the curve of the earth. Then the trunks of the palms and those of broad-boled forest trees rose over the curve, then white beaches. Kayangel, the only true atoll in Palau, is the northernmost land in the archipelago. The canoes touched there, turned, and raced back, this time coasting down the east shore of Babeldaob. The canoes touched again at Airai, then raced on to Pelelieu and the other islands of the south.

The last of the big *kaep* races occurred in 1875, just before the arrival of the first Spanish administrators. No Palauan alive today remembers what those races looked like.

The days of sail are over in Palau, but they have left their impression on the Palauan language. *Muchut el yars*, 'old sails,' is the Palauan term for lineages with ancient origins outside the village. The 'sails' of the saying belong to the canoes imagined to have brought the first members of that line. *Beches el yars*, 'new

Kapingamarangi fisherman in outrigger canoe, barrier reef, Ponape,
Federated States of Micronesia.

Paddling canoe and clothesline, Moen Island, Truk,
Federated States of Micronesia.

sails,' is the term for lineages with recent origins outside the village. *Emeched el bekall*, 'tacked sails,' describes a navigator capable of sailing close to the wind, and by extension any leader capable of guiding his people through hard times. *A redil a desemelel a sechal*, Palauans say, 'The woman is outrigger to the man,' and they call a bride *beches a desomel*, 'a new outrigger.' *Ngkora terib sel a daob*, 'Like foam on the ocean,' describes something that goes on and on without end or resolution.

The biggest canoe in Palau was not a sailing vessel at all. It was the *kabekl*, the gigantic paddling canoe in which Palauans went to war. Useless for subjugating peoples of far islands, it was the perfect warship for attacking those cousins across the channel. The hull of the *kabekl*, like that of the *kaep*, was hewn from *Serianthes grandiflora*, the great tree the Palauans called *ukal'l*. With the war canoe, only the largest trunks would do, for the hull was from 48 to 58 feet long. As with the *kaep*, the war canoe's thwart bars extended beyond the hull on the outrigger side. Lashed longitudinally to the underside of the bars was an outboard paddling platform of bamboo poles which allowed the *kabekl's* paddlers to work double banked. The largest canoes carried as many as 32 paddlers.

The paddles, painted red, were 4.5 feet long, with a short handle and a long, lanceolate blade for which they were called *besos*, also the word for 'spear.' Hornell speculates that more than just the common shape may have inspired the double meaning – that the paddles may once have been used as weapons.

The *kabekl* now lives mainly in museums and in the plates of old German tomes, but the war canoe's memory, like that of the *kaep*, lingers on in the language.

*Ngkora besos Lechemai, el dingariou el meritch*, 'Like the paddle of Ngerechemai, breaking on the downstroke,' goes the Palauan proverb. The origin of the saying is this: At one time the men of Ngerechemai, a village on Koror Island, were the best paddlers in all Palau. They had a special stroke, a secret way of digging hard, fast, and deep with the paddle, then pivoting the handle forward and bringing the blade smoothly up. The stroke looked effortless, yet the Ngerechemai canoes left all others behind.

The secret was closely guarded. (Palauan villagers would rather spill it to the ethnologists or even, I suspect, to the *Russians* than to the spies of a neighboring village. Several years ago, a scientist I know spent months in Palau gathering information on traditional fishing techniques. The fishermen, he found, were not much concerned that their secrets might appear someday in a book. What worried them was that the scientist might pass secrets on to the fishermen of the next village. Until the scientist promised not to convey anything to cousins across the channel or over the hill, he learned no nuances of hook-baiting or secrets of chumming).

Competitors from other villages were puzzled by Ngerechemai's racing success, until someone noticed that Ngerechemai paddles often broke on the downstroke. That observation led to experimentation, and the secret was out. Soon everyone had mastered the method. *Besos Lechemai*! shouted captains from villages all over Palau, *Paddles Ngerechemai*!, and the crews mimicked perfectly the stolen stroke. The proverb applies to any secret technique that comes to light.

Each war canoe was built by a *dachelbai*, or master builder. It was purchased from him by the village and kept in a canoe house, or *diangel*, made by and purchased from another *dachelbai*, a master who specialized in canoe houses. (One of the more nicely conceived of Palauan customs was that no one used articles made by his own hand. Non-specialists could maintain the village war canoe and the canoe houses, but were not supposed to build them. By this simple device, some long-forgotten social planner encouraged those refinements in skill that come with specialization and at the same time stimulated a continuous flow of money and goods through the community.)

The *kabekl* hull was inlaid intricately with shell, painted red, rubbed with coconut oil, and polished with dry coconut husks. The shell designs varied, and here, in the art of inlay as in all endeavor, Palauans competed. On one *kabekl* in the British Museum, the motif is a mother-of-pearl bird, a reef heron, apparently, which is repeated at intervals along the hull. The necks of all the herons crane forward in the direction of attack. In another war canoe, which J.S. Kubary saw in 1895, the hull was divided into a checkerboard by mother-of-pearl strips, with the nacreous operculum of a *Turbo* shell at the center of each square.

When a *kabekl* went to war, festoons of egg cowries and other shells were suspended from all the thwart bars, from the prow and stern, and from various places on the outrigger platform.

The outrigger platform had a floor of cane laid atop the two stout booms attaching the outrigger float to the main hull. Over the hull, as a kind of continuation of the cane platform, was a wooden 'bridge.' On raids, the canoe's captain sat on the cane platform and shouted orders to the paddlers. Abreast of him, on the wooden bridge, stood the chief warrior, the commandant of marines. His spearmen clustered at the middle of the canoe, with one able fighter at the bow, and the best warrior of all stationed on a narrow bamboo platform projecting forward from the outrigger platform. It was this warrior's job to cut off the heads of slain enemies and hang them from the outrigger. He and his colleagues were walking arsenals. They carried 12-foot spears with shafts of bamboo and points of hardwood, the points transversely barbed, so that the friendly hand withdrawing them did more damage than the belligerent hand that had sent them in. They carried slings for casting two-foot darts with reasonable accuracy up to 60 feet. In-fighting, they used eight-foot spears, sword-clubs inset with razor-edged shells or sharks' teeth, wooden slip-on knuckles studded with more sharks' teeth, and bamboo daggers.

*Ngkora cherabrukl el diblsiochel e reborb*, 'Like the lobster, bedecked with weapons,' goes a Palauan proverb. 'Like the Palauan, armed to the gills,' might be the lobster's answer.

It must have been something: a war canoe flying at you, 32 paddles flashing red in the sun, then singing through the water, the paddlers straining in perfect rhythm, the red hull glistening with oil, the pearl inlay prismatically refracting the light, the white festoons of cowries and the dark decapitated heads swaying with the beat, the tattooed, ululating warriors bedecked like lobsters with spears, swords, and redeployed sharks' teeth. What went through the heads of the cousins across the channel, on seeing that? I believe I might have been inspired to head for the hills.

*The islanders, no longer independent, have ceased to build the 'kaep' and the*

Pieced wooden canoe hull, Truk,
Federated States of Micronesia.

Outrigger brace, Carolinian sailing canoe, Saipan,
Northern Mariana Islands.

'*kabekl*', writes James Hornell in *Canoes of Oceania*, the bible of Pacific canoes. The bible, in this instance, is no longer correct. The *kaep* is extinct, it's true, but the Palau Islanders, after an interval of 60 years, have once again begun building the *kabekl*.

The first of the new canoes was built by the people of Ngchesar district on Babeldaob, and their example was followed immediately, Palauan competition being what it is, by their neighbors in the district of Airai.

I was in Palau in 1980 when the Airai war canoe was receiving its finishing touches. I visited the tin-roofed boathouse where the canoe rested; I walked several times around it; I missed entirely its significance.

The boathouse and the country around it were deserted, except for one young Palauan man asleep in the canoe behind his dark glasses. He woke once, glanced at us sleepily, mumbled something, and went back to sleep again. The canoe itself was not enormously impressive. It was lacking decapitated heads, of course, and there were no festoons of cowries. The hull was not yet painted, but it had received its inlay of shell. The workmanship, it seemed to me, was cruder than it had been in the old days. The holes carved to receive the inlay did not match the shape of the shell with especially fine tolerance, and the edges of the wood were rough. It was probably to be refinished later. The canoe's motif was a moray eel in mother-of-pearl, and I liked that well enough.

Several days later, at a restaurant in Koror Town, I began to gain some understanding of the true dimensions of the boat I had walked around.

Palau Culture Week was underway, and I was having lunch with one of its organizers, Katherine Kesolei, director of the Palau Community Action Agency. Moses Sam, another of the organizers, entered, saw us, and sat at our table. (He was once the fastest man in Micronesia. As a sprinter at the Micro-Olympics held in Ponape in 1953, he won the 100 yard dash in 10 seconds flat, a remarkable time in an athletic era of bare feet, tennis shoes, and terrible tracks.) Today Moses was excited. He had just come from a meeting at which the launch of the Airai canoe had been planned, and he unveiled an elaborate scheme for us, sketching it on the page of my notebook.

The canoe, he explained as he drew, was named *Kesebekuu*, which meant moray eel. Sixty years before, a war canoe named *Kesebekuu* had been the last and most famous war canoe ever built in Airai. It had never participated in a war, Sam said. Airai was not a warlike state. Its people were noted for their skill at politics, a skill forced on them by geography. A buffer state between the powerful antagonists Koror and Melekeok, Airai required political cleverness of its leaders, Moses said.

The original *Kesebekuu* had never needed to go to war, but as a racing canoe it had won often, Moses said. It had been destroyed in World War II. In the long American siege of Babeldaob, the Japanese had chopped it up for firewood. The new *Kesebekuu* was a little shorter than the war canoes of the old days, just 43.5 feet long. The people of Airai had been working on it for five months. Racing, it held 20 men. In war, should Airai ever have to go to war again, it would hold 30.

*Here's the K-B Bridge*, said Moses, pointing to his drawing of the new bridge that joins the islands of Koror and Babeldaob. He showed us where, on the day of the launch, the shallow water on either side of the deep channel would be fenced off with poles hung festively with coconut leaves. Behind the poles, on the Koror side, people would park their boats. Spider shells, crafts, and local foods would be on sale on the Koror side, and on the Babeldaob side, hot dogs and soft drinks would be sold from booths.

*The boxes of T-shirts have just arrived*, he said. *They came out real good. There's a moray eel on the front. For the paddlers we have red headbands decorated with moray eels.* Moses paused and with his pencil tapped cautiously on his sketch of the bridge. *How many people live in Koror? Seven thousand?* he asked Kathy Kesolei. *We'll have to check with the engineers to see how many people that bridge can hold.*

Here, it seemed to me, Moses was getting way ahead of himself. He was thinking much too big. The Koror-Babeldaob bridge, the longest single-span bridge in the world, according to Palauans, is Palau's greatest modern engineering achievement. It seemed inconceivable that Palauans would want to gather in sufficient tons of humanity to damage the structural integrity of the bridge, just to see a 43.5 foot canoe. There are only about 15,000 Palauans in the universe. By my own rough calculation, you could pile the entire Palauan race on the bridge and it would hold. I glanced at Kathy Kesolei, a pragmatic woman whose sense of proportion I trust. But nothing in her expression revealed that she found Moses's calculations out of line.

*The canoe will be preceded by speedboats*, he said. *They'll all come fast. The war canoes really* move. *With the Ngchesar canoe, a 25-horsepower speedboat couldn't catch up with it. Finally the paddlers got tired, and the canoe got to shallow water, which means more drag on the hull, and the 25-horsepower caught up.* He shook his head at the memory of that speed, then continued. *On the bridge, policemen will be marching back and forth, and . . .*

*Why?* asked Kathy Kesolei. Her tone was dry, I·thought.

Moses heard the dryness, too. It slowed him down for a moment. He didn't know why, he said, but that was the plan.

*The police will fire a 21-gun salute*, he continued. *There will be seven trumpets . . .*

With this fanfare of trumpets, I began to get the idea. The *kabekl's* depth was greater than the four-foot figure Hornell gave in his book. The war canoe's displacement in the Palauan psyche was far more voluminous than its displacement in the water.

\*     \*     \*

The Palauans may have contemptuously called it a 'dish', but the sailing canoe of the central Caroline Islands was in fact a finer vessel than any of their own. The 'flying proa', as canoes of the Carolinian type were first called in English, was probably the finest canoe ever made.

The birch-bark canoe of the American Indian was a beautiful vessel. It was admirably suited to the streams and lakes on which it was paddled. The ocean, though, is a sterner test. More was demanded of ocean-going canoes, and more art went into them.

The skin-covered *kayaks* of the Eskimos and the *baidarkas* of the

Lee and outrigger platforms, Satawal Island sailing canoe, Saipan,
Northern Mariana Islands.

Carolinian sailing canoe moored in lagoon at Chalan Kanoa, Saipan,
Northern Mariana Islands.

Aleuts were ocean-going canoes, and they were superb. In their *kayaks*, Alaskan and Canadian Eskimos negotiated the sea ice and narrow leads of the Arctic Ocean, and Greenland Eskimos threaded the unpredictable seascape off their island, wending their way through Manhattans of ice. In their *baidarkas* the Aleuts paddled a Pacific far colder and more chronically violent than the more pacific Pacific of the Micronesians, thousands of miles to their south. But skin boats were mostly coastal craft. They were designed for hunting sea mammals and sea birds, not for long, open-ocean crossings. The skin boats of the North – *kayaks*, *umiaks*, and *baidarkas* – were not so much inventions as they were plagiarism of the plans for sea mammals. The skin canoes, like the mammals, had an inner framework of ribs, sometimes wooden, but often simply lifted from the skeletons of sea mammals. The skins stretched over the boat frames formerly had covered sea lions, walruses, and bearded seals. If simpler is better, then the sleek skin boats were the best canoes ever. If ingenious is better, then the flying proa was best.

The double canoe of Polynesia is probably the finest of canoes, if your requirements are those, say, of Noah. If your requirements are those of Ulysses or Leif Ericson or Sir Francis Chichester, then the flying proa is finest.

The flying proa was such a good idea, or combination of ideas, that it spread with little change throughout most of Micronesia. It was not just a low-island technology. Flying proas were found in the high islands of Yap, Truk, and the Marianas, as well as the low islands of the Marshalls, Gilberts, and central Carolines. The islanders of all these archipelagos spoke mutually incomprehensible tongues, yet their flying proas differed only in nuances – small divergencies in outrigger lashing here, sail rigging there. The canoe-builders of one group or another might have been tempted to make an improvement, had there been anything to improve. There was not.

The subtlest of these inventions, and the one which probably most offended the aesthetic sense of the Palauans, is the asymmetric hull. In cross section, the outrigger side of the proa's hull – the weather side, since Micronesian canoes always sail with the outrigger to the wind – is more rounded than the lee side, which is nearly vertical. The drag on the outrigger tugs at the canoe's weather side. In canoes with symmetrical sides, like the *kaep*, the prow wants to come off course. The asymmetry provides a counter influence. When a flying proa's asymmetrical proportions are correct, the canoe, given a push, sets off straight and true.

The flying proa impressed every European seaman who saw it.

*I do believe they sail best of any boats in the world*, wrote Captain William Dampier, the buccaneer. *I did here for my own satisfaction try the swiftness of one of them; sailing by our log, we had 12 knots on our reel, and she ran it all out before the half-minute glass was half out; which if it had been no more, is after the rate of 12 miles an hour; but I do believe she would have run 24.*

But the best evidence as to the quality of the canoe, more telling than any approval by old European sailors, is that it endures. The flying proa still flies.

All the other great canoes of Oceania have vanished: the Marquesan outriggers with necks like swans; and the Ellice Island outriggers with bifurcated prows carved to resemble the open mouths of kingfish; and the Samoan canoes with figureheads carved into sawteeth; and the Tahitian double-hulled traveling canoe, *tipairua*, with its tall, nearly vertical figureheads carved like totem poles with small *ti'i* figures and surmounted by a large *ti'i* figure; and the Cook Island outrigger with a stern post carved like the Devil's tail; and the Tahitian outrigger canoe called *va'a motu*, with its odd balance platform along which crewmen ran to windward when the wind rose; and the 100-foot, double-hulled Tuamotuan voyaging canoes with twin masts and vast platforms joining the two hulls along their entire length, vessels designed with great Tuamotuan intelligence but built with poor Tuamotuan wood, their hulls a mosaic of odd planks sewn together with sennit; and the 100-foot war canoes of the Maoris, with figureheads 18 feet tall and carved, by the finest artists in Oceania, into complex perforated patterns of vortices, swirls, scrolls, and sometimes into grotesque human faces with mother-of-pearl eyes and tongues sticking out at the enemy; and the catamarans of Mangareva, great modular rafts holding 100 men or more, which, on drawing near Captain Beechey, the first European to see them, detached themselves from one another, becoming a fleet of smaller catamarans carrying 20 men; and the punt-shaped, square-ended canoe-rafts of the Chatham Islands, propelled by oars instead of paddles, hulls 50 feet long yet built of tree ferns, flower stems, and kelp bulbs, in the Chatham Islands' absence of any sort of suitable timber; and the Tongan *tafa'anga* with its odd-looking multiple outrigger booms; and the small, rude, but precious canoes of the Easter Islanders, who, separated from the Polynesia of their ancestors, lost first the wood suitable for voyaging canoes and then the knowledge of how to build them, and who ended by paddling on surf boards made of rushes, or just swimming, out to greet their visitors; and the Fijian *thamakau*; and the Gilbertese *baurua*; and the *taurua* of Rapa; and the *foulua* of Niue, have all vanished.

Only the flying proa survives. Smaller than in former times, but identical in design, the Micronesian outrigger canoe still hangs on in a handful of islands in the central Carolines. On two of those islands – on just two of the thousands of Pacific Islands that once boasted great navigators – live knowing men who still make long, compassless, open-ocean voyages under the triangular sail.

Carolinian boy relearning lost sailing skills in Satawal Island canoe, Saipan,
Northern Mariana Islands.

Lateen sail, Satawal Island canoe, Saipan,
Northern Mariana Islands.

# Navigators

The best navigators in Oceania, during the period of first contact with Europeans, at least, were the Micronesians. The best of the Micronesians were probably the Marshallese and the central Carolinians.

The voyaging canoes of those two Micronesian groups were nearly identical. Both had double-ended hulls that were asymmetric in cross section. Both had sharp keels and big lee platforms. There were small differences in ornamentation, the Carolinian canoe having a forked prow ornament at either end, a wooden bifurcation that was supposed to represent the forked tail of a frigate bird; the Marshallese canoe having ends that were unadorned or ornamented by figureheads shaped like axe blades. There was a minor structural difference in that the *wa lap*, the voyaging canoe of the Marshallese, lacked the forked-Y outrigger connectives employed by the Carolinians. But the only real divergence was invisible. It was a divergence in guidance systems. The onboard computers-in-loincloth of the two craft were programmed differently.

Marshallese and Carolinian navigators sailed under the same heaven, of course, and they had the same panoply of guiding stars to choose among. The various Marshallese atolls lay under stars different from the Carolinian atolls', and the navigators of the two archipelagos picked different stars and constellations as their references, but they used them in much the same way.

It was the universe below the canoe that was truly different. A difference in waves made for the difference in navigators. The Caroline Archipelago is oriented east-west, and its islands, lying on that axis, do little to interfere with the regular east-west swells prevalent in the north equatorial Pacific. The Marshalls, oriented north-south and more tightly clustered, break those swells into more complex patterns. Marshallese waters are on the one hand more chaotic, and on the other contain more information, once a navigator learns to decode it.

To teach the science of swells, the Carolinian instructor arranged stones and pebbles on the floor of the men's house or on the sand outside. To teach the more complicated swells of Marshallese waters, the Marshallese instructor employed stick charts. Marshallese instructional or mnemonic charts, called *mattang*, were made of the midribs of the leaflets of coconut fronds. The chart-maker curved the strips to represent the deflection of the swells by the presence of an island. Where curved strips intersected, the student could expect confused seas. That 'confusion' would unconfuse him, for to the Marshallese navigator, turbulent patches of ocean were the most informative, the surest indications of where he was. In the framework of curving and intersecting midrib swell lines, islands were sometimes represented by cowry shells. The stick charts were meaningless without the instructor on hand to explain them. Each chart was designed according to the individual requirements of the teacher, its maker. It charted only Marshallese waters, and was useless anywhere else. The charts had, and have, no equivalent in the classrooms of European navigation, for the phenomenon they marked, and upon which Marshallese navigation depended, was scarcely noticed by European sailors and was never analyzed by them at all.

The Marshallese recognized four main swells. They were *Non Rear* or *Rilib*, the 'Backbone Swell,' which was the strongest and came from the east; *Kaelib*, the western swell, weaker and harder to detect; *Bundockeing*, the weak swell from the north; and *Bungdockerik*, the strong swell from the south. Each swell, on striking an island, was deflected back in the direction it came. In interpreting this backwash wave or 'land wave,' the Marshallese were masters, probably the best in the Pacific, though the Gilbertese and Tikopians were good at it, too. Leeward of an island, a Marshallese navigator could detect the land wave for more than 20 miles, and windward for as much as 50.

Twenty years ago, one of the last Marshallese navigators, Raymond DeBrum, explained swell interpretation to an American interviewer:

*Each different kind of wave has its own name in Marshallese. First of all, there are the long easterly 'main waves' which cross from one atoll to another. They are known as 'steady waves' because they do not break into shorter waves. These long, even swells are known in Marshallese as* non rear.

*Then there are the shorter waves which cross the long waves at certain*

*points out from an atoll. In Marshallese they are called* drilep. *The* drilep *change direction according to the location of each atoll. Near an island or atoll, the* drilep *cross the longer waves at an angle of about 45 degrees on both sides of the land. The point where the* drilep *and the* non rear *meet is called* buoj, *which is Marshallese for 'knot.' There will be a 'buoj' on each side of the island. It is at the 'buoj' that the waves are seen fighting each other, so it is easy to recognize a 'buoj.' This is the point where one goes to find direction if he is off course or lost.*

*Going out from one atoll in a ship or smaller vessel, one meets many cross-waves coming in to land. These 'coming-in' waves are called 'jimin ba.' Those going out toward another island are called 'rekitlek.'*

*The farther the boat goes away from the land, the more nearly parallel the shorter wave, 'drilep,' gets to the main wave,* non rear. *But as the sailor comes near to another atoll, the cross-waves come closer to making a 45-degree angle with the main wave, so as the boat approaches the atoll or island, the skipper knows both by the direction of the waves and by the feel of the vessel, that an island is near, because the main wave is bouncing his boat over toward the land and the cross-waves are pushing it toward the island also. He feels both of these.*

*The prevailing winds in the Marshalls are easterly. If a sailor is on the eastern side of an island, he will meet the cross-waves coming toward him, and he will have a pitching feeling, bringing him in toward land. At the same time there will be a big side-rolling caused by the main wave, the steady swell. If the motion from the east is stronger than from the south, he must tack – turn about and follow the cross-wave until he locates the 'buoj' – and then put himself in its inside corner, and head directly away from that corner.*

This problem, approaching an island from the east, was one of many the Marshallese solved simply by scrutiny of the sea around him. For the Marshallese navigator, the sea's surface was as full of headlines, notes, and comment as the European captain's newspaper was to him. The Marshallese was as literate in swells as the European was in tide tables, compass readings, and charts.

The Marshallese could read in the dark. The look of the waves was less important than the feel of them, day or night.

*These elder skippers first of all would take the younger man out to the ocean,* wrote Raymond DeBrum in 1962. *They would be in a boat, but they would lay the young man in the water, on his back, and tell him to float*

Sunset, Sokehs, Ponape,
Federated States of Micronesia.

Managaha Island view, Saipan,
Northern Mariana Islands.

*and relax so that he would get to know the feel of the waves as they came along.*

What, I wonder, was it like for that young man?

Was the student distracted by a sense of the blue, miles-deep void under him? Or was the importance of the lesson, and the grave attention of the old men in the canoe, such that he kept his mind on the problem – on the wind-sculpted surface of the void and the difficulty of understanding its motion? Was recognition slow and cumulative, or did it come in a flash? What was the moment like, when the sea finally spoke to him?

It is a wonder that the fine discernments required of the Marshallese navigator could be taught at all, passed from one man to another. But who was the brown Einstein who first looked into the confusion of the waves and saw the equations there?

As important to Marshallese navigation as the navigator himself was the Marshallese weatherman. The weatherman could read the sky as lucidly as the navigator could read the sea. The family who owned the weather knowledge and the family who owned the navigation system were seldom the same.

*Checks and balances,* explains Tony DeBrum, Raymond DeBrum's nephew and presently the Minister of Foreign Affairs for the new Republic of the Marshalls. *But the two families had to work together. They couldn't afford a split. All the good navigation in the world won't help you if you can't tell the weather.*

One navigator who managed to learn more than was customary about weather was Joachim DeBrum, Raymond's father. Joachim was a Marshallese da Vinci; a boatbuilder, doctor, businessman, and artist as well as navigator. The weather, though it was supposed to escape his attention, did not. In his fine hand in a thin notebook, Joachim set down some particulars of Marshallese weather interpretation, and long after his death, his son Raymond made them public.

(Raymond made a little *too* much public. In Micronesia, specialized knowledge is not intended for everyone – it is private property of the families who own it – and the secrets of navigation are the most closely guarded of all. *Raymond broke tradition, the son of a bitch,* Tony DeBrum told me, with a smile half fond, half irritated, 20 years after Raymond's indiscretion. *But it's all right, he did it in such a way that he didn't reveal too much.*)

The damage has been done, so here is a selection from Joachim's notebook:

If the dull-colored cloud called *kero laninbwilwa* appears at zenith near sunset, in four days there will be squalls.

The cloud called *lilab,* 'old woman cloud,' a large, serrated northern cloud, means very squally weather.

If the clouds called *neirere,* red morning cirrus, appear near the sun, they foretell breezy weather, and perhaps rain. (This is like our own less specific, more melodramatic *Red sky at morning, sailor take warning . . .,* which is about all we have in this line.)

*Tibeb,* a bank of southern stratus clouds, ugly looking, may mean nothing at the time, but indicates heavy weather in three or four days.

*Kero kimiji,* the 'palm cloud,' is formed something like a palm leaf – a cirrus with slender filaments stretching out from it. If this cloud is moving eastward, and if there is any thick cumulostratus at east-northeast or thereabouts, it will rain heavily in approximately six hours, or perhaps four hours, especially if this cloud is enlarging.

If *kero arenbaw,* the 'shark-teeth cloud,' a dull-colored cloud, is seen at the north at sunset, the wind will be fair at midnight.

If *akin wom,* 'crab finger' clouds – small puffs of cirrus – are seen at dawn near the sun, it means that breezes will remain. (These cottony puffs are imagined to feed the sun.) If they are seen at night, expect fresh breezes. If the weather is calm and any of these puffs appear, they will travel toward the sun, and a breeze may be expected from nine o'clock onward.

If the evening sky is overcast, yet a star appears at zenith, one may go torchlight fishing. As the tide turns, though, it will rain.

If the base of *kero wan,* the cumulo stratus, is not level, and the eastern part is lowest, the breeze will remain strong.

If a greenish-white cloud shaped like a dog's head appears with its nose pointed east, with very fine cirrus blown about it, and if this dog's head cloud seems to be heaping up, in 30 hours the wind will shift to the southeast.

If heavy rain has fallen for a couple of days, every *bata*, 'rainstorm,' will have a *lum*, 'afterstorm,' even though a *lur*, 'dry day,' intervenes. Sometimes a long *bata* has a small *lum*, while a short *bata* may have a large *lum*.

And so on and so on.

Traditional Marshallese navigation, if not exactly dead, is certainly comatose. There are men alive in the Marshalls who still know how to navigate by reading the waves, but they don't do it any more. The Marshallese have become expert builders of schooners and other modern vessels. For indigenous Marshallese navigation to revive – for Marshallese men and women to put to sea again in sailing canoes, guided by the *buoj* and *drilep* and *non rear* – would probably require the total collapse of Western civilization.

In the central Carolines, however, traditional navigation is alive and well. In the islands and atolls of Pulap, Elato, Lamotrek, Ifaluk, Tamatam, Pisaras, Pulusuk, Puluwat, and Satawal are navigators who make star-guided voyages in sailing canoes. For the most part, these voyages are short, 40- or 100-mile trips to turtle islands or to close neighbors. But on two islands, Puluwat and Satawal, navigators are once again making voyages of 500 miles and more in outrigger canoes. Carolinian navigation, instead of dying peacefully, is in the middle of a renaissance.

The origin of the renaissance is interesting. Two white men, without intending to, figured in it.

The first was Thomas Gladwin, an American anthropologist who came to Puluwat in 1967. Gladwin wanted to find out how non-Western people think. His concerns were the concerns of most American social consciences active in that period. He suspected that the Puluwatans, like poor people in the United States, would do badly in foreign tests of intelligence. Puluwatans were not poor – poverty was not a concept in Puluwat's cultural repertoire – but neither did they come from college-educated families. Going entirely outside the American culture, studying the thought processes of Puluwat, might be a way to get a fresh look at an American problem. That, at any rate, was Gladwin's rationale, and it won the support of the National Institute of Medical Health. It made perfect sense; it was a good idea. It certainly wasn't an idea new to anthropology. I wonder, though, how much the allure of the islands had to do with Gladwin's decision to go there.

It doesn't matter. Whether the analogy of Puluwat was ever applicable to Appalachia or the ghetto, Gladwin's book on Puluwat, *East is a Big Bird*, is the best portrait yet of the society of the Carolinian navigator and his art.

Puluwat was beautiful, even for a coral atoll, Thomas Gladwin found. Puluwat's five islands are more tightly clustered than the islands of most atolls, and greener. Two of the islands, Puluwat and Allei, are big, with large taro gardens and plenty of wild forest left standing. The Puluwatans are not crowded, as are, say, the Satawalese. The entire population of Puluwat Atoll lives on Puluwat Island, with room for more on that island alone. A big bay in the inner shore of the inhabited island serves as a harbor for sailing canoes, and they can be moored there in any weather short of a typhoon. The island is broad enough that its inner margins are protected from high winds, and the breadfruit trees grow gigantic and tall. The breadfruit canopies, like those in a climax jungle, steal all the light, shading out secondary growth and making a cool, dim, spacious understory in which the Puluwatans go about their business. The houses, of concrete or plank or thatch, sit between the huge trunks of the breadfruits. The people, Gladwin found, though notorious elsewhere in the Carolines as pirates, in their home islands were spontaneous, friendly, and polite.

Voyaging is the drama that keeps Puluwat's Eden from being bland. It provides fiber and tone for the life. It allows, Gladwin believes, for a heroism in which every Puluwatan can participate. Boys and girls go to sea as young as five or six, and opportunities abound for them to go voyaging throughout the rest of their lives. Not everyone can qualify as a navigator, but every Puluwatan knows enough to work as crew. Crewmen are heroes too.

*There are discomforts of course, and also risks,* writes Gladwin. *Without them there would be no zest, and no occasion for heroes. But the discomforts are transitory and, when you are used to them, quite tolerable. The risks are real, but not nearly as great as one would expect contemplating*

Ant Atoll off Ponape, Ponape,
Federated States of Micronesia.

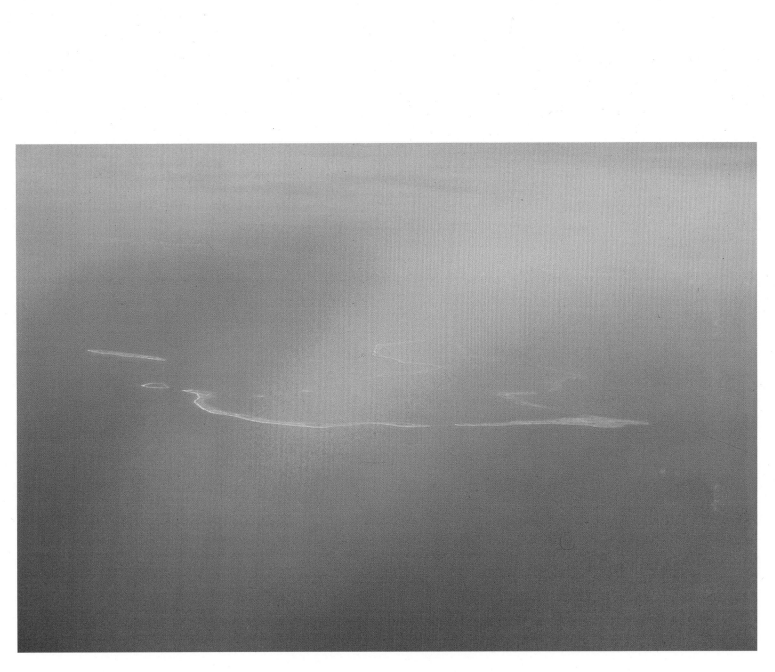

Rainbow, Ulithi Atoll, off Yap,
Federated States of Micronesia.

*the vast stretches of ocean, the tiny slivers of wood and cords which are a canoe, and the little dots of land which are the islands to which Puluwatans sail.*

Voyaging, as Gladwin and others before him have pointed out, rescues places like Puluwat from provincialism. Without it, Puluwatans would be forced into endless commerce with themselves.

There are theocracies in the world, and oligarchies, and monarchies. Puluwat is a navigarchy. Navigators on Puluwat have more stature than chiefs. The navigator's position is so secure on the atoll that he feels no need to pose, or to dominate others, or to act aloof. Navigators are not like admirals; they don't mind getting drunk with the crew. At sea, the navigator's command is informal. He listens to the suggestions of others. The sheet, though, is in his hands, and decisions, when all is said, are his.

Gladwin's instructor in the art was the great navigator Hipour. A greater navigator lived on Puluwat, the elderly Ikuliman, the most masterful of the master navigators and canoe-builders of recent history. Ikuliman retained all his faculties, but he had lost all his teeth, and Gladwin had trouble understanding him. The anthropologist and all his informants had to converse in Trukese, which was a second language for both parties, and communication was difficult enough as it was. Of the navigators Gladwin met, Hipour was easily the best explainer.

Hipour was then in his mid-40s, a short, stocky man with sun-darkened skin, a large and impressive head, and hardly any neck at all. His hair was cut Puluwat style, short on the sides, piled high on top. His eyes were calm and humorous, his ears pierced for the insertion of shells or flowers. On his thighs were tattoos of leaping dolphins, along with one bit of unintentional decoration, a scar from a shark. The deltoid muscles of his shoulders were tattooed with the spreading rays of a rising sun, his biceps with various symbols more abstruse. He had started his training as a navigator late – his father had not taken him to sea until he was eight – but he had surmounted that.

Before the instruction began, Gladwin had to promise that his book on Puluwat navigation would not be so detailed that a reader could navigate by it without further instruction. That was an easy promise for Gladwin to make; any book that complete, he estimated, would require many volumes, and he was writing one.

Hipour and Gladwin sat at a table across from each other, a chart of the Carolines between them. (The idea of a chart – a two-dimensional representation of the ocean – was foreign to Puluwat. Hipour, who was illiterate, had never used one, yet his knowledge of the subject, and his acute Puluwatan spatial sense, were such that he quickly learned to read the various symbols for islands, reefs, and soundings.) In front of Gladwin was a typewriter, and as Hipour spoke, the anthropologist tapped out his words on the machine.

*As time went on,* Gladwin writes, *each of us became familiar with the thinking of the other so we could borrow analogies from the other's system to develop a point, but I believe we remained throughout true to the logic particular to each of our traditions.*

*The consequences of this, which probably should not have surprised me but nevertheless did, was that I found there were very large domains in which we were inclined to process information by identical logics, even though we might sort it into different kinds of cognitive boxes. At the same time there were ways in which he surpassed me, and others in which I went beyond him. In some perceptual modes, such as sensing the direction of waves or the presence of reefs deep below the surface, Hipour could work with discriminations I not only could not perceive but could scarcely conceive. For my part I was able, indeed eager, to explore in my mind the implications of novel and imaginary relations between facts, relations which to Hipour (I felt) were meaningless simply because they were not real or useful.*

Carolinian navigation shares few points in common with celestial navigation as practiced by Europeans, not even points of the compass.

The 'star compass' by which Hipour and his Carolinian colleagues sail happens to have 32 points, like the magnetic compass of Europe, but the points lie at different, less even, intervals around the circle. The North Star, Polaris, marks north on the Carolinian compass. The Southern Cross in its upright position marks south. The cardinal direction for Carolinians is east, and it is marked by the star Altair, which Carolinians call 'the Big Bird.' In the quadrant between north and east, the steering points on the star compass are the rising positions of the Little Dipper, the Big Dipper, Cassiopeia, Vega, the Pleiades, Aldebaran, and Gamma Aquilae. The steering points between north and west are marked by the setting positions of the same five stars and constellations. The steering points in the southern hemisphere are the rising and setting positions of Beta Aquilae, Orion's belt, Corvus, Antares, Shaula, and the Southern Cross in five different positions.

Today many Carolinian navigators use magnetic compasses, but only as auxiliary aids, usually to maintain course in daytime. They don't completely trust magnetic compasses and are quick to ignore a compass if its intuitions run contrary to their own. Carolinians subscribe to the Tongan proverb, *A compass may go wrong, but never the stars.*

The thing about the star compass that most confused Gladwin, puzzling him for most of his stay on Puluwat, was what he took to be the vagueness and inaccuracy of its steering points to north and south. The northern steering constellations of Big Dipper and Cassiopeia both cover a lot of sky; they overlap, in fact. Ward Goodenough, who had studied Carolinian astronomy in the 1950s, in his scheme for the star compass picked one star in either constellation to represent it. His choice was arbitrary. He simply chose two stars that gave bearings evenly spaced along the horizon. When Gladwin presented Goodenough's two stars to Hipour, and later to Ikuliman, the two navigators denied that these were the correct stars to use, then disagreed between themselves as to which stars *were* the correct ones. Hipour, confused by the whole line of questioning, had to consult his old teacher, Apwi, before returning with the answer that disagreed with Ikuliman's.

To the south, Gladwin felt, the star compass seemed almost as blurry. All five of the most southerly steering points were marked by the Southern Cross in different positions. The first point was the Cross at rising, when it lay on its side; the second, the Cross once the rotation of the heavens had lifted it to a 45-degree angle; the third – due south – the Cross upright; the fourth, the Cross in decline, once again at a 45-degree angle; the fifth, the setting

Cross, lying once more on its side – the other side this time.

The obvious difficulty is that only one of the five points can be occupied by the Southern Cross at a given time; the other four are vacant. What if your island of destination lies due south, under the upright Cross, but the Cross at the moment is horizontal, only just rising? What if the Cross has not risen at all? (For a good part of the night, it lies below the horizon.)

The answer, Gladwin found, is simply that the star compass is indeed inaccurate to north and south. The Carolinians do not require 360 degrees of uniform accuracy from their compass. The star compass is only as accurate as it needs to be to get a canoe to its destination. The thousand-mile band of ocean familiar to the Puluwatans runs east–west, and most navigation is along that axis. The eastern and western steering stars are the important ones. For the most part, north–south voyages are short and require less refinement of the system.

On a return trip by night with Hipour from Pulusuk to Puluwat, a voyage of 60 miles, Gladwin found himself falling into the Carolinian way of regarding the heavens.

The basic course for this trip was slightly west of north, toward the setting of the Little Dipper, but a westward current was running and a northeasterly wind blowing. Hipour, in compensation, was steering north, toward the North Star. (A Carolinian navigator must be able to judge the pace and direction of the wind and current. Having determined those, he refers to his memorized instructions for the alternate star to steer by, given this amount of current set or that amount of wind drift.) Clouds lay along the horizon – trade-wind cumulous clouds most often do in the tropics – and they frequently obscured the North Star. (In the Carolines, just north of the equator, the North Star lies low, close to the horizon. The Carolinians call it *Star that never moves* but just as easily could call it *intermittent Star*, so often is it hidden behind clouds.) The Little Dipper on the night of Gladwin's voyage was frequently obscured too, but the Big Dipper stood high and bright in the sky.

*The two 'pointer' stars of the Dipper showed where the North Star was hidden,* writes Gladwin. *I soon became used to how the Dipper lay and*

Rock Island, Palau,
Republic of Belau.

Rock Island (*Elabaob*), Palau,
Republic of Belau.

*unthinkingly shifted my attention from the North Star's projected position to just the Dipper alone in gauging when we were on course or off. Then I realized that in this northern part of the sky, where all the significant stars are more or less bunched together, it is not necessary to have a discrete point on which to set a course. Instead, to borrow an expressive image from the Mississippi River pilots of Mark Twain's day, you steer by the shape of the sky. You are sailing into a part of the heavens, not towards a dot of light.*

Gladwin's other large difficulty was in coming to terms with the Carolinians' conceptual scheme for organizing their information. In the universe of the Carolinian navigator, things are topsy-turvy: islands move about and the canoe holds still.

Hipour and Gladwin's other informants never said this in so many words – they were not accustomed to spelling out their conceptualization, never having felt the need among themselves – and Gladwin is not certain he has it exactly right, but the scheme works something like this: The canoe, once it has left shore and is on course toward its destination island, ceases to move. Everything else moves. The stars travel through their customary arcs above, the ocean and its islands slide away beneath, Puluwat retreating behind, the destination island advancing from ahead. The canoe sits still.

For any sailor traveling in a small boat on a big ocean, the vessel becomes the emotional center of the universe; for Carolinian sailors it becomes the conceptual center as well. While the canoe is on its correct 'path' to the destination island, it is conceptually immobile. If a gale should blow the canoe off the path, or, if in passing over one of the underwater banks that serve the navigator as seamarks, the canoe should digress in pursuit of fish, it is then thought to move. Returning to the path, it becomes stationary.

The concept of the moving island is useful in two of the more important and ingenious aspects of the Carolinian system: first in the navigator's use of 'reference' islands to determine distance traveled, second in tacking.

The reference-island system is called *etak*. For each course between a pair of islands in the Carolinian system, the navigator's instructions provide him with an *etak* island – a reference island. Ideally, the *etak* island makes the third corner of an equilateral triangle for which the islands of departure and destination make the first two, but it seldom works out so perfectly. As the voyage progresses, the navigator mentally follows the 'movement' of the *etak* island under the steering stars. He never *sees* the island – it doesn't really have to exist – but he knows its location. On a southeastern voyage, for example, he 'watches' the *etak* island pass first under Gamma Aquilae, then under Aldebaran, then the Pleiades, then Vega, then Cassiopeia, then the Big Dipper. As the island arrives at each new star, a new *etak* – a new leg, or segment – of the voyage begins. The *etak* system provides no new information; it is simply a way for the navigator to mark off distance he has traveled. *Etak* relieves some of the strain on the computer in a loincloth.

In tacking, a navigator makes similar use of an invisible moving island. In this case, the reference island is his island of destination. On each tack, the navigator mentally follows the 'progress' of the island under the steering stars in the quadrant where it lies, thereby dividing into segments the distance covered on the tack, and at the same time keeping track of his destination. Here again, no new information is added, just new pigeonholes for it. The moving island aids the navigator in his dead-reckoning – in his ceaseless, sextantless appraisal of his canoe's position.

Hipour and his teacher, and his teacher's teacher, and all the teachers of the hundred generations of navigators before them, knew that the islands did not really move. But they spoke of them as moving, and the conception worked.

The Carolinian navigator sets out, Thomas Gladwin discovered, with no overall plan for his voyage. Puluwat's sailing canoes were all scrupulously maintained, ready to sail at a moment's notice. A moment's notice was often all they had. *I'm going to Pikelot. Who's going with me?* a Puluwat man would shout, toward the end of a drinking party. If he was not too drunk, others would join him, and a canoe, or canoes, set forth on the hundred-mile trip to Pikelot, Puluwat's turtle island.

The plan for any Carolinian voyage unfolds as conditions dictate. *The navigator,* writes Gladwin, *has in his memorized sailing directions a whole portfolio of instant plans.*

The navigator sets out on the greatest ocean with no tools but his brain. His only gear is a preternatural development of his intuitive sense of the speed of his canoe, of the set of current and wind, and of the motion that the swells impart to his craft. His memory banks are crammed with star courses, alternate stars, back-up screens of islands, or screens of underwater reefs, or screens of birds, that will catch him should he miss, and volumes of other data fed in by the hundred generations of navigators that preceded him. To his memory he refers all problems. He is a more startling demonstration of mind than any supertanker captain on his bridge, or admiral on his atomic carrier.

*       *       *

The second white man to figure in the Carolinian renaissance was a New Zealander, David Lewis.

Lewis grew up in Polynesia, on Rarotonga, in the Cook Islands. Rarotonga in those days had separate schools for Maori and European children, and Lewis's parents sent him to the Maori school. *I will always be grateful,* he has written. *The sallow white children had to wear shirts, shoes and socks and sometimes even pith helmets, while we trailed our toes luxuriously through the warm road dust, clad only in shorts or pareus.* Lewis preferred the company of Maori children, and diving on the reef with them. He preferred coral cuts and urchin spines in his bare feet to the restriction of shoes. *My education, in strict academic terms, left something to be desired,* he admits. *Even then, I rather suspected some fallacy in our Niuean teacher's assertion that 42 and 24 were the same thing. But many things that I learned were beyond price. Not least were the ancient sagas to which I listened enthralled . . . of legendary heroes like Kupe, the reputed discoverer of New Zealand, and of other fabled voyagers.*

*'He waka ururu kapua' – 'A canoe to dare the Clouds of Heaven' – was the* karakia *or prayer of the captain of the great canoe Kura-hau-po before he guided it across two thousand miles of ocean in Kupe's wake. Such traditions are poetic reflections of former reality rather than literal history, but men like Kupe really did exist. They truly 'dared the clouds of heaven,' and theirs was not the least page in the story of seamanship.*

Rota,
Northern Mariana Islands.

Former U.S. airstrip, Tinian,
Northern Mariana Islands.

Lewis overcame the mathematics of the Niuean teacher sufficiently to graduate in medicine from Leeds University in 1942, and to practice medicine until 1964. In that year, his shadow education in the old Polynesian sagas won out, and he quit his practice for the sea. His attempt to circumnavigate Antarctica in his 39-foot ketch *Isbjorn* was worthy of Kupe or any of the other legendary navigators. It was, depending on one's philosophy about margin of error, a bold or a hare-brained adventure. In his *Ice Bird*, Lewis wrote it up. In another book, *We, the Navigators* (1972), Lewis set out to do for indigenous navigation in the entire Pacific what Thomas Gladwin had done for Puluwat.

In 1968, the year after Gladwin visited Puluwat, Lewis began a 13,000 mile voyage around the tropical Pacific, searching out those islands where traditional Pacific navigation was still practiced, or at least remembered. The Central Carolines, where indigenous navigation was liveliest, was an inevitable stop. In 1969, he showed up on Puluwat in *Isbjorn* with an introduction to Hipour from Thomas Gladwin. Lewis asked Hipour if he would be willing to navigate Lewis's ketch, without compass or sextant, using only traditional methods, from Puluwat, in the Carolines, to the island of Saipan in the Marianas. That had been a common voyage in the old days, but still it was a journey of almost 500 miles, and as nearly as anyone could figure, no one had made it in a traditional manner for 65 or 70 years. Traditionally was the only way Hipour knew how to navigate. He quickly agreed to the plan.

Lewis stowed his compass, sextant, charts, radio, and wristwatch, and *Isbjorn* set out in stormy weather late one afternoon. Hipour's immediate destination was the customary first stop for this voyage – the uninhabited island of Pikelot, 100 miles northwest of Puluwat. From there they would make the 450-mile crossing to Saipan.

As he left Puluwat, Hipour took careful backsights at his home island, and from these judged the set of the current. In the central Carolines there are three strong currents. The North and the South Equatorial Currents nearly meet there, both flowing west. Between them, flowing east, is the Equatorial Counter-Current. This triple belt of moving waters is continually shifting north or south, with great eddies sometimes forming between. Shifts in direction and speed of the current are unpredictable and sudden. The consequence, for navigation, is that in the Carolines the alternate steering stars of the navigator's memorized instructions became indispensable. As *Isbjorn* drew away from Puluwat, Hipour saw that a strong current was setting the vessel north. For a current like that, his instructions informed him, the correct star-compass point to steer for was the setting position of the Pleiades. He headed that way.

At 11 that night, the Pleiades set. Hipour was by then familiar with where, on this heading, the North Star and the stars of the Great Bear aligned with various parts of the ketch's rigging, and he held course by maintaining that alignment.

Shortly before dawn, Lewis noticed a bright star unfamiliar to him, and he asked what it was. Ulutak, the translator, relayed the question.

*Satellite*, Hipour answered, in English. The Stone Age navigator grinned.

In mid-morning, after 100 miles of navigation by stars and swells, Hipour made a perfect landfall on the 500-yard-long island of Pikelot. It was an insignificant feat, by Carolinian standards. As Thomas Gladwin has pointed out, Puluwat navigators regularly make that trip while intoxicated.

From Pikelot, after waiting fruitlessly for the weather to improve, *Isbjorn* set out for Saipan. Their destination, Hipour told Lewis, lay just left of the setting position of the Little Bear. That was not, however, the constellation that would guide them. Hipour's instructions told him he would encounter a strong westward-running current for the whole trip, and they referred him to another star. If winds had been moderate, that star would have been Polaris, the North Star, but because a strong wind was abetting the current, one was to steer for the rising position of the Little Bear.

Hipour had never made this voyage – the last Puluwatan navigator to sail to Saipan had done so decades before Hipour's birth – yet, trusting without qualm the reliability of his instructions, he set off in a direction where he knew his destination

wasn't. He did not find this at all remarkable. There were far longer and trickier star courses filed away in his memory. He knew the way to the Philippines, if he should ever want to go. He knew the way to islands that were no longer even there.

*This was a six-day voyage*, Lewis writes. *At the start Hipour was uncertain whether the swells would be familiar. He gazed intently at the sea for hours on end, noting the direction, wavelength, frequency, height and profile of the swells, until the pattern was recognizable day or night; the individual swells had become as familiar as the faces of his friends.*

Hipour had instantly recognized 'the Big Wave,' the swell that runs from under the Big Bird in the east, but the others required those hours of study. When Hipour had them all down pat, he pointed each one out to Lewis.

*Isbjorn's* wake was making a 15-degree angle with the direction she was headed. A glance sternward at that 15 degrees gave Hipour her leeway angle. He explained that to Lewis, emphasizing the point by laying pencils at the proper angles on the chart table. (Hipour by now was perfectly comfortable with charts. They were no use to him in navigation, but they were helpful in educating anthropologists.) *As to speed*, writes Lewis, *Hipour, to my chagrin, was soon able to estimate it better than I could – despite my 20,000 miles in Isbjorn.*

On the fifth morning out from Pikelot, they saw seabirds, one of the land-indicators by which all Pacific navigators 'expand' their targets. In late afternoon, they sighted Farallon de Medinilla, an island 50 miles north of Saipan. This was part of a second 'screen,' the Marianas Archipelago itself, a long, north-by-northwestern-trending arc of high volcanic islands, a safety net to catch any slightly errant navigator who misses any particular island in the chain. At noon the next day they reached Saipan.

Returning to Puluwat, Hipour and Lewis had better weather. The screen that caught *Isbjorn* this time was composed of the submerged reefs and nearly contiguous bird zones that surround Puluwat's low neighboring islands of Pikelot, West Fayu, Satawal, and Lamotrek.

Four days after leaving Saipan, they encountered that screen. *The first flock of birds appeared at noon*, Lewis writes. *It was a sizable one,*

Prow, Mokilese boat, Ponape,
Federated States of Micronesia.

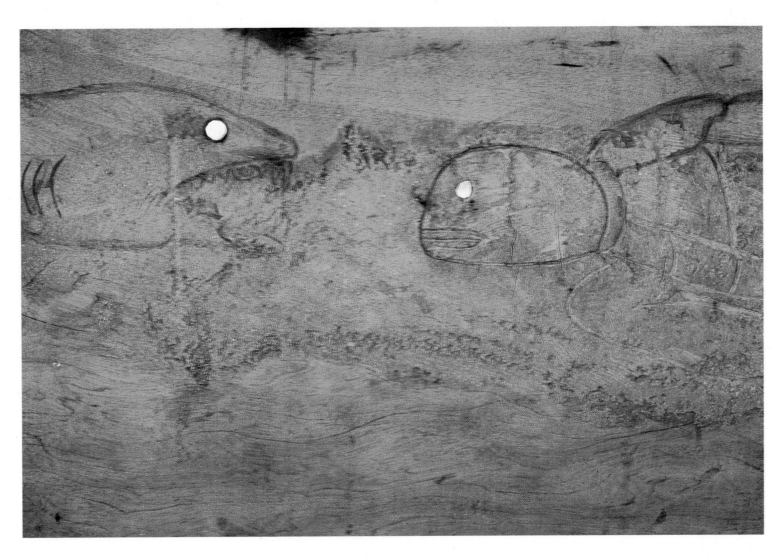

Moray eel and war canoe, detail from Airai war canoe, Palau,
Republic of Belau.

*consisting of nearly a dozen terns and one or two noddies. All were fishing industriously.*

*Half an hour later we sighted a bigger group of 20, mostly noddies this time. Then at 17:30, as evening approached, the event we had so anxiously been awaiting took place: two birds broke off fishing to fly away low and straight south-by-west. In the next 30 minutes five more ceased circling and diving and flew off in exactly the same direction; then a single bird, next a pair. All headed south-by-west or 190°. There could be no further doubt. We had arrived in the bird zone of Pikelot. Landfall on this occasion was by terns and noddies. There were no boobies.*

*Hipour and Ulutak's tense watchfulness now relaxed completely. Such birds as were still circling about were now regarded only as indications of shoals of fish. A fishing line was put over the stern and Hipour gaily spun the wheel and set off in pursuit of the nearest swooping flock — without a care for the course he had previously been following so meticulously. It was hard to realise that this mood of relief and celebration after four days and 450 miles of steering only by the stars, sun, and waves with never a sight of land, had been induced by the behaviour of a few score tiny seabirds.*

Later Hipour explained. Pikelot, he said, lay between 10 and 20 miles off, in the direction the birds had taken. Had the distance been less than 10 miles, *Isbjorn* would have seen the island. Had it been more than 20, there would have been fewer birds or none at all. The distance was probably closer to 10; the high number of birds suggested a low number of miles.

The sailors paused half a day on Pikelot, then continued to Puluwat, arriving after dark the next day. A bonfire guided them through the pass in the reef. As *Isbjorn* entered the lagoon, coconut-rib torches suddenly blazed along the entire margin of the bay in the inhabited island. The ketch was surrounded by paddling canoes, and Natives swarmed the rail, shouting their congratulations.

None of the participants guessed it at the time, but Hipour's 900-mile round-trip voyage would prove epochal.

Several months after *Isbjorn* had left Saipan on her return voyage, Martin Raiuk, the paramount chief of the island of Satawal, fell ill and was sent to the hospital on Saipan. Recovering on Saipan, Chief Raiuk heard talk of the Puluwatan exploit, and it must have bugged him. In the Central Carolines, and thus the entire Pacific, Satawal is Puluwat's chief rival in excellence of navigators, and Puluwat is Satawal's. The chief had conversations with Dr. Benusto Kaipat, a leader of the enclave of Caroline Islanders that had existed on Saipan for centuries, and the two men discussed the possibility of future voyages. The Carolinians of Saipan were interested in such voyages both from straightforward racial pride and for reasons more intricate. Renewed voyaging between the Carolines and Saipan in sailing canoes, they thought, would help strengthen the Carolinian claim to Saipan. (When the ancestors of the Saipanese Carolinians first arrived on that island, it was uninhabited, the Spanish having forced the evacuation of all the Chamorros, the original inhabitants, to Guam.) Martin Raiuk returned to Satawal full of ideas about voyaging.

In 1970, two of the best navigators on Satawal, the half-brothers Repunglug and Repunglap, rose to the Puluwatan challenge. The Repung brothers set sail with three crewmen from Satawal to Saipan. The canoe was 26 feet long and provisioned with 60 pounds of taro, somewhat less breadfruit, and a pile of drinking coconuts. All 400 inhabitants of Satawal saw the voyagers off.

Like the trip from Puluwat to Saipan, the Satawal-Saipan voyage begins customarily with a trip to a turtle island. Satawal's turtle island is West Fayu, 52 miles to its north. Repunglug and Repunglap covered that first leg in 10 hours. They waited on West Fayu four days for favorable weather, and when the wind shifted to southerly, they departed, steering for the setting position of the Little Dipper. They were sailing north, into that part of the star compass that Gladwin had found to be vaguest, but they were untroubled. Neither of the half-brothers had ever sailed this course before, nor had their instructors, their respective fathers, who had taught them 30 years earlier; yet the brothers trusted in their instructions – in their recollections of the mnemonic songs that showed the way.

Late the first evening, when their instructions sang to them that the time was right for it, they altered course from the setting of the Little Dipper to the North Star.

On the third day, high winds forced them to drop the sail. The canoe wind-drifted from its correct path to Saipan, and for the first time in three days of sailing, in the Carolinian conception of things, the canoe began to move. It did not stray far, however, for a characteristic of the outrigger canoe is that with sail down, the outrigger positions itself upwind, lessening the drift and indicating the drift's direction. (The outrigger points like a needle in the direction the canoe is being pushed.) A Carolinian navigator, on raising the sail again when the wind ceases, usually assumes he is in roughly the same position as when the storm began.

On the fourth day out of West Fayu, the Satawalese sighted Saipan. Neither of the Repung brothers had ever seen that high island, yet they knew the Carolinian names for all the passes in Saipan's reef, having learned them at the knees of their fathers. The Satawalese arrived, on purpose, at the village of Chalan Kanoa, one of the principal Carolinian communities on Saipan. They made landfall in daylight. Had it been night, Repunglug said afterward, he would have negotiated the pass in the reef anyway, having memorized, 30 years before, the stars that marked it.

Since the voyages of Hipour and the Repungs, the Puluwat-Saipan and Satawal-Saipan voyages have been repeated many times, as have voyages from the Carolines to Guam. In 1975, a canoe navigated by Repunglug showed up in Okinawa. The Carolinians of Saipan now have two voyaging canoes from the Carolines, one a full-sized, 26-foot canoe from Puluwat, the other a 16-foot canoe from Satawal. The big canoe was intended for the Bicentennial's Tall Ships festivities, but never made it, and rests now at the Saipan airport. The small canoe, which was swamped almost continually on its voyage up from Satawal, rests weekdays on the beach at Chalan Kanoa, and on weekends it sallies forth to fish beyond the reef. The vessel's name is *U-drive*. On it, certain Carolinian men and boys on Saipan, long out of touch with their tradition, are once again learning to sail the Carolinian way.

It may seem more than improbable, in this age of wallowing dreadnoughts, but the flying proa may again fly widely in Micronesia. Knife-edged hulls may soon slice Micronesia's blue swells and triangular sails may again lean before the wind on Micronesia's blue horizons.

Net-fisherman and boy, Kosrae,
Federated States of Micronesia.

Woman and child, Truk,
Federated States of Micronesia.

# Fishing

The strategies by which Micronesians pull fish from the sea are nearly as varied and polychromatic as Micronesia's fish themselves. The ingenuity, persistence, and humor with which the Micronesian matches wits with fish flow from a reservoir as deep as the ocean he fishes in. There are those, like James Hornell and Louis de Freycinet, who argue for the canoe as the apogee of Micronesian material culture. These men tend to be sailors and biased. A better argument could probably be made for the Micronesian tackle box. Enthusiasm for voyaging is dead or dying in many of the islands; enthusiasm for fishing is not.

The fishermen of the Marshalls, whose land resources are the poorest in Micronesia, are among Micronesia's best fishermen.

*The Marshallese do so much fishing that they've differentiated all kinds of techniques, even though some of the names are for very similar methods*, says Bill Pululoa, a Hawaiian who directs the Marshalls' fisheries program. Pululoa's own people are busy fishermen themselves, and marine science is his field, but he was not prepared for the nuances in fishing technique and nomenclature he has found in the Marshalls. *They're like Eskimos*, he says. *How many different names do Eskimos have for snow? The Marshallese are the same way about fishing.*

For an example, Pululoa described fishing the *tongue-and-groove* system at the edge of the reef – the spurs, or fingers, of coral that project oceanward from the reef flat, and the sandy valleys between the fingers. *Just before you reach the tongue-and-grooves, you come to holes in the reef flat. There's one name for fishing the holes. If you continue on and fish the groove, there's a separate name for that. If you walk farther out on the tongue, there's another name for that.*

*Diil* is the Marshallese name for fishing for squirrelfish in small holes on the reef during low tide, using a two- or three-foot-long leader fastened to a piece of wood of about the same length. *Kiijball* is hanging onto the reef while spearing. *Katooj* is hunting lobsters or coconut crabs when the moon is right. *Tilkawor* is hunting lobsters at night with artificial light. *Rrwe* is inserting the bare hand into holes and crannies in the reef and searching for fish. *Okwa* is pole-fishing from a raised platform or tripod. *Dentak* is striking needlefish with a club or a paddle as they float on the surface on moonlit nights. *Kokkojekjek* is trolling inside the lagoon. *Irarak* is trolling outside the lagoon. *Koddapilpil* is fishing with a handline from a canoe on the deep ocean for fish other than tuna. *Latippan* is fishing for tuna. *Pelok* is line-fishing while your canoe drifts with the wind and current inside the lagoon. *Apep* is using woven brown coconut fronds to catch sardines as they are chased ashore by bigger fish. *Kokkaalal* is waiting along the usual path of fish on the reef, usually at the beginning of ebb and flow tide, to spear them. *Kaajrabol* is pole- or line-fishing without bait, just jerking the line in hopes of hooking a fish. *Kotaltol* is chasing mackerel into a throw net held upon one side. *Kojjaromrom* is line-fishing at night by jerking the line to cause phosphorescence that will attract fish to the bait. *Kadjo* is pole-fishing for goatfish. *Kojolim* is using a weighted hook baited with octopus, and dragging it along a sandy bottom. *Ttoor* is pole-fishing from the beach. *Juunbon* is pole-fishing at the reef edge at low tide or on dark nights. *Tilkomera* is fishing at night with a torch and machete. *Kolojawil* is fishing for bonitos. *Kommak* is fishing for needlefish. *Jibke* is fishing, or mammaling, for dolphins. *Kottoor* is chasing fish into a weir. *Rupe om* is line-fishing inside the lagoon using hermit crab for bait. *Korkaak* is trolling at night. *Aejek* is using a surround net on dark nights. *Jaak* is using a diving mask to watch the fish so that one can jerk the line when it strikes. *Jabuk* is daytime fishing along the reef ridge with a long net.

*A good fisherman is held in very high esteem*, says Bill Pululoa. *In the old days, the great fishermen traveled from atoll to atoll to challenge the fishermen there. The famous fisherman would sail in and settle on some kind of wager. They used bamboo poles at night on the reef. Each guy had his special lures and rods. They would walk out together, then walk in opposite directions on the reef. They were like pool sharks.*

*Pool sharks?* I thought, as I jotted this down. I tried to imagine what species of shark would frequent tidepools. Then I realized that Pululoa meant billiards.

*Merrick de Brum was one of them*, Pululoa was saying. *He used to travel around in a schooner, challenging people. Marshallese fishermen lost a lot of face if they lost.*

The fishing techniques these duelists practiced are supposed to have originated with a group of beings called *Nonieb*. The *Nonieb*, who follow the old Marshallese way of life, live contemporaneously with 20th-century Marshallese, but in a separate world. Occasionally someone from the anti-universe of *Nonieb* crosses over. A Marshallese fisherman will meet a *Nonieb* fisherman on the reef, and a friendship will form between them. The anti-fisherman comes to trust the fisherman. In time the fisherman learns *Nonieb* secrets.

It was the *Nonieb*, presumably, who informed the Marshallese that the species of big-eyed squirrelfish called *mon* is most active when the moon is full and the tide is low; that it is best to fish for them when the moon is not obscured, because the squirrelfish need the light to see the bait; that a sinker about the size of the top joint of your finger is best to bring the bait down to them; that the squirrelfish, though it has a poisonous spine that can paralyze a hand, never has toxic flesh, like so many Marshallese reef fish; and that it is good food for babies. The *Nonieb* taught the Marshallese various ways to call fish magically. They helped the Marshallese compile a catalog of the various things a fisherman could throw in the water to attract fish.

*Nonieb* chemists taught the Marshallese how an extract of the plant the Marshallese call *wop* and Europeans call Barringtonia could be used to stupify fish. *Nonieb* advisors taught the inhabitants of the small island of Mejet, which has no lagoon, how to convert small groupers into big yellowfin tuna. The groupers hatch on Mejet's reef by the millions in certain years; the people catch them, cook them, take baskets of them to the reef edge, and chum for yellowfin, drawing those great pelagic fish right in to their shores.

If it was the *Nonieb* who taught Marshallese to catch flying fish by attracting them to the light of coconut-frond torches, then it was the Marshallese themselves, I suspect, who adapted Honda generators to the same purpose.

Marshallese catch flying fish in daytime, according to a veteran fisherman named Lajuar Hax, with bait made from the legs of ghost crabs. They peel the exoskeletons from the legs, bait either end of the line, and skip the white legs across the surface behind the boat. The legs run across the ocean with the wraithlike speed

Boy with reef fish, Ponape,
Federated States of Micronesia.

Ponapean family fishing, Ponape,
Federated States of Micronesia.

at which, in life, they skittered over sand. An energy-saving modification of this method is called *rejeb*. The fisherman makes floats out of 10 or 15 coconuts, attaches a short length of line to each, baits the hooks with crab legs, scatters them on the ocean, and returns in an hour.

Marshallese catch rabbitfish with no tools at all. When rabbitfish are plentiful on the reef, those big marine herbivores can be herded, like sheep, by as few as two men. The two fishermen, canny as sheepdogs about the habits of their flocks, splash on either side, directing the fish up on the beach, where they kill as many as they need and let the rest go.

In the Marshalls, as elsewhere in Micronesia, it is the improbable methods that seem to delight people most.

*How did the Nonieb ever think of that?* the old-fashioned Marshallese seem to be asking of these methods, if I read their smiles and head shakes right. *How did our ancestors ever dream that up?* more modern Marshallese seem to wonder.

*We catch rainbow runners with a rope,* says Joe DeBrum, manager of the airfield on Majuro Atoll, the Marshallese capital. *It's a method that came I think from Jaluit. It's a good method. It was community fishing. You would go around to four or five guys, and everybody would jump up and go out. Now you go by the guy's house, he's had two, three beers. He says, 'Why don't you go yourself?'*

At first, according to Joe, people believed this method, called *ekkoonak*, would work only with a special kind of sennit, but it turned out that Japanese rope was just as good. Fishermen stationed themselves at intervals along the rope and with it they encircled a school of rainbow runners. For some reason, the fish refused to pass under the rope. Once the school was inside the ring, the men could walk it into shallower water. The fish obligingly followed them anywhere, unwilling to swim under the rope. The men tightened the ring, then waded in and scooped up the fish with nets. The rainbow runners saw their schoolmates enter the nets and disappear, but still refused to brave the rope and escape.

*If the school is too big, you can split them up by throwing a rope across the middle,* says Tony DeBrum, Minister of Foreign Affairs for the Marshalls and the younger brother of Joe DeBrum.

(The DeBrums are a remarkable and ubiquitous lineage in the Marshalls. They are descended from Anton DeBrum, a Portuguese copra planter who, with a colleague named Capelli, bought the atoll of Likiep, married Marshallese women, and started the DeBrum–Capelli line, which would become the Marshallese Rockefellers, Kennedys, Fords, and DuPonts, all rolled in one.)

*The half of the school you didn't need, you let go.*

*The rope you used with rainbow runners was called 'iia,' which happens to mean rainbow. It's a funny coincidence of languages.* (The Marshallese word for rainbow runner, *ikaidik*, makes no reference to a rainbow.) *When you surrounded the rainbow runners, you splashed water to frighten them and keep them inside. There was a special word for 'splashing water by throwing rocks.' You didn't just say 'throwing rocks.'* (Tony DeBrum, while a student in Hawaii, was one of the principal compilers of the excellent PALI-series Marshallese dictionary, and Marshallese words are still on his mind. It was from his dictionary that I lifted the earlier list of Marshallese fishing terms.)

As a boy on his home atoll of Likiep, Tony, the lexicographer-and-foreign-minister to be, took shark rides.

*It was like a sport,* he remembers. *It's good, a lot of fun. They don't do it anymore. It happened annually or twice annually on Likiep, as part of a celebration.*

*You catch a bird and you throw it out, not quite dead, with a hook in it. It flutters, and the shark hits it. You sit on the wide, green part of a palm frond, like a sled. The shark pulls you down to one end of the beach. You turn the sled around, and the shark pulls you back to the other. Every kid is trying to get his own shark. He's trying for the fastest ride, and the longest. When the shark got tired, you called an elder over and he killed it.*

Of all the odd fishing techniques, the one that seems to have impressed Marshallese most was their way of catching dolphins with sound.

*We catch them with canoes,* explained Lajuar Hax, contending the mammal was in fact a whale. *There's maybe three guys on the canoe. Ten canoes, maybe. We dive down maybe five feet, all three of us, or sometimes just two. When the 'captain' points down with his paddle, we know we're gonna dive. Everyone dives in all the canoes. Underwater, we hit two rocks together. The whales are gonna hear it.* Hax pointed to his own ear. *They're gonna scare.*

The animals, according to Joe DeBrum, were in fact dolphins, and the divers went down eight to 15 feet. The line of canoes fenced the dolphins against the inside of the reef. The divers all knocked their rocks together a couple of times, and at the noise, the dolphins jumped. The clicking of the rocks was to find out where the animals were, as much as to scare them. The canoes then advanced, forming a tighter semicircle around the dolphins. *When the one,* says Joe, *the leader, they call it the 'queen' or the 'king,' jumped up on the sand, then all the others jumped after it.*

Hax and DeBrum disagree on the identity of the sea mammal. It is possible that the technique they describe was used against both dolphins and whales. Joe DeBrum's home atoll is Likiep, Lajuar Hax's Ailinglaplap. It could be that residents of the former hunt dolphins, the latter whales. But it seems more likely, from Hax's description of the animal's length and DeBrum's of how it strands itself, that for both atolls the creature was a pilot whale.

\*     \*     \*

The atolls and islands of the central Carolines, like those of the Marshalls, are poor in terrestrial resources and rich in fishermen. Carolinian fishermen practice many of the same techniques that the Marshallese do. They go after flying fish, for example, with the same coconut floats, the only difference being that they bait them not with ghost-crab legs, but with pieces of coconut meat. The Carolinian fisherman would understand most of what his Marshallese equivalent was up to, and vice versa, but there are, at the same time, areas of specialization.

Because the central Carolinian island of Satawal is small, scarcely a mile long, with only a half square mile of reef to fish, its inhabitants have become experts at trolling the deep water off their island for the small tuna called skipjack.

*When we get into the school of tuna, we sail the canoe down, following the same street the tuna have taken,* Lino Olopai, a former Satawal resident, explained to me. *Then the old man in the back of the canoe will dip water from the canoe and splash it on the ocean to get the tuna excited. He says some magic words. The tuna start to jump, and he splashes some more water. Finally he tosses the hook overboard. The old man hauls in maybe one, two, or three fish, then he says okay — it's all right for everyone to start fishing. The old man is the expert. He's responsible for making sure of the tuna. Because, say, if someone hooks the tuna and gets it to the boat, and that tuna falls off, then the rest of the tuna will follow that wounded tuna down, and we're gonna lose the whole school.*

Most Micronesians now troll in speedboats, which bounce the lures along pretty fast, and that was the only kind of trolling I had done in the islands. In my ignorance I asked Olopai if there was an advantage in trolling at the slower speed of a sailboat. Did you catch different species when going slower?

Olopai gave me a look to see if I was serious. *Oh, you go much faster in a canoe,* he said. *The canoe is faster than a motorboat. And it is quiet. It doesn't scare the fish.*

Michael McCoy, director of Marine Resources for the Federated States of Micronesia, is another former resident of Satawal. He served as a Peace Corps Volunteer on the island, and he has a Satawalese wife. On the walls of his office in Ponape hang pearl-shell lures made by his father-in-law for skipjack fishing on Satawal. The lures are beautiful. To the concave side of each pearly spoon, lashed in place with sennit, is a turtle-shell hook.

The day I visited, McCoy leaned back in his office chair, remembering Satawal. He is a big, gruff American in his mid-30s. His person, like his walls, is Satawalese in decor. He is tattooed all over in the traditional Carolinian style. Running up his legs, where the uniform stripes would be on pants, are broad bands of blue-black designs. On the backs of his hands are arrows. At first glance the backs of his hands look like the backs of dollar bills, where the American eagle grips a bundle of arrows in its claw. At second glance the arrows don't look the least bit American. They're Carolinian arrows. They may not be arrows at all, in fact. The barbs of the point spread at oblique angles, like those of Micronesian fish weirs. McCoy's hands look warlike, but they may simply show peaceful fishing scenes.

*The Satawalese are probably the best in the world at pelagic pole-and-line*

Young fisherman, Ponape,
Federated States of Micronesia.

Stone fish weir on reef, Yap,
Federated States of Micronesia.

*fishing for skipjack,* McCoy said. *You use pearl-shell lures. A sailing canoe, poles, line, and eight or nine guys. It's probably the best fishing on Satawal. You don't throw any bait. The splashing and the motion of the outrigger pounding down in the water and coming back up produces a lot of froth and attracts the fish. They just come up right behind the boat. No bait, no nothing. The pearl-shell lures are fantastic. The fish are small skipjack and you pull them in, 'whissst whissst.' When the fish are runnin' and the wind's blowin', you can bring in a ton, a ton and a half. 'Whissst whissst,' 500 to 600 fish in the canoe at a crack, two or three pounds apiece. You're screaming and jumping up and down. It's the most fun I've ever had in my life.*

The inhabitants of Yap, the high-island cluster at the western end of the Carolines, besides being excellent fishermen, are astute folk-scientists of fish. Yapese marine taxonomists employ a classification system totally unlike the system of Linnaeus and the West. The Yapese classify a fish according to its home range, habits, taste, and smell, not according to the number of gill slits or the affinities of the caudal peduncle. A Yapese marine biologist, nibbling at a specimen, can tell by the taste whether it inhabited the reef flat, or whether it ate algae, even if he has never seen or heard of that species before.

Yapese marine biology is an applied science. The Yapese biologist's study of fish often goes beyond the purely practical, but he and the Yapese fisherman are always the same man.

The Yapese have a reef-zonation scheme nearly identical, except for the names, to the scheme employed by Western ecologists. First, fringing the land, is a green belt of mangroves called *melil.* Next comes the shallow offshore depression called *lupuu,* which is full of algae; then the slight rise of the sandy plateau called *ey;* then the descending slope called *tele makeff,* a zone of corals and seaweed; then the moderately deep channel bottom called *makeff;* then a seaward *tele makeff,* ascending this time; then *lane yan,* the reef flat, a zone dotted with seaweed and coral; and finally the *naa,* the zone where the surf breaks on the coral boulders of the reef ridge. Beyond is *regur,* the deep ocean. *Daken e dai* is the ocean's surface zone, *toru wan dai* the midwater zone, and *t'ai e regur,* the ocean floor, or what we would call the benthos. Each of these Yapese zones has its different species of

fish – or its characteristic mix of species, since some travel between two or more zones. The Yapese fisherman knows where to go when he wants what he wants.

In Yap there are genus names and species names for fish. The bump-head parrotfish is of the genus *choi* and the species *gamegul.* The blue parrotfish is genus *choi,* species *galunglung.* Sometimes in Yapese, as in scientific Latin, both names are the same. Damselfish are genus *dak,* species *dak.* Sharks (all species but the hammerhead) are genus *aeeng,* species *aeeng.* The hammerhead has an order all its own, and that, for an animal built so anomalously, seems sensible.

Applying their marine science, the Yapese once used fishing lines of twisted hibiscus fiber that could hold 300-pound fish, nets of hibiscus fiber with support ropes of sennit, floats carved of the light wood of hibiscus, lures of feathers or fish skin or young coconut leaves, hooks of hawksbill-turtle shell, and diving goggles of transparent turtle shell glued into wood frames with breadfruit sap. Today, for the most part, the lines are nylon, the nets monofilament, the hooks steel, and the diving goggles glass and synthetic rubber.

Seaward of the *ey* zone, the Yapese build enormous stone weirs called *ach,* in which they trap *ey* fish at low tide. Smaller but similarly shaped weirs of mangrove poles and bamboo panels were formerly built in the *lupuu* zone. The mangrove used was *Rhizophora mucronata,* which resisted wet rot. The Yapese also built small, portable fish traps of mangrove and bamboo which they covered with coral, disguising the entrance and catching reef fish that fled there for refuge. They build the same style of trap now, but metal rods usually take the place of the bamboo and mangrove.

Bottom-fishing for the parrotfish they call *nmam,* the Yapese use a live land crab for bait. They tie the crab's legs to its body and lower it into 30 or 40 feet of water just off the reef. As the crab descends, it emits a stream of bubbles, which attracts the parrotfish and causes it to strike. The technique may seem over ingenious, but the reward can be ponderous, for parrotfish of the species *nmam* grow to five feet in length and 300 pounds.

The fish the Yapese call *wachamul* is caught with bait from the trocus. Catching it requires attention and a light and educated hand. The *wachamul*'s cautious habit is first to blow on the bait, then to take it in its mouth, then to spit it out again. These subtle underwater happenings are telegraphed through the line, to those who know the code. The Yapese fisherman is not fooled by the fish's first blow. He strikes in the instant that the bait is in the fish's mouth.

*Wachamul* fishing is a nice illustration of the difficulty of much subsistence skill. How many generations did it take the Yapese hand to learn to decipher those slight tremblings of the line? If the Yapese hand ever lost its intelligence, how long would it take to relearn it?

In the old days, the Yapese torch-fished at night in sailing canoes. The canoe most favored was the big *mar e magal*, sometimes 40 feet long. Flying-fishermen had to be good sailors, and young men trained in shallow water by balancing themselves in paddling canoes, which their friends rocked to simulate ocean waves. The Yapese charted and named the various paths a flying fish might take in relation to the canoe. The erratic course of a flying fish was not, to the Yapese, erratic. The fisherman knew how to predict those rapid, sharp-angled dartings just under and above the surface, and with his long-handled nets he seldom missed.

Trolling in sailing canoes, the Yapese caught bluefin and yellowfin tuna, mahimahi, wahoo, barracuda, sharks, swordfish, and marlin. On hooking up with a swordfish, they strung a mat woven of coconut fronds on the line. The mat slipped backward until it came to rest over the swordfish's eyes, and the fish ceased to fight so hard. These coconut-frond blinders also worked with marlin, though not so well.

The Japanese, during their occupation of Micronesia, destroyed all the big sailing canoes to prevent the Yapese from sailing around to other islands. Now the Yapese go trolling and torch-fishing in speedboats or in outrigger paddling canoes powered by outboard engines. The swordfish blinders are made of store-bought cloth.

\* \* \*

The people of Fais, an outer island in the Yap system, are specialists in catching sharks.

They are the only people in the outer islands of Yap to do so. In much of Micronesia, shark-eating is considered unseemly. In Western civilization we don't eat much shark, either – not knowingly, at least – but the Micronesian feelings against shark are different and run deeper. Riding in small boats with Micronesians and freshly caught sharks, I have heard them joke and complain about the odor, when I smelled nothing at all – or nothing but a standard fishy smell.

Mike McCoy, who has lived here and there in Micronesia, thinks he has a partial explanation:

*In Satawal, people are buried at sea. They know damn well that the sharks eat 'em. Satawal was only Christianized in the 1950s, after the war. Almost everybody remembers burying people at sea, weighing them down with rocks in burial mats, and seeing big sharks tear the mats open.*

*In the Marianas there are more sharks than anyplace. There's an unbelievable potential for a shark fishery there. Not long ago they caught an 18-foot tiger shark off Saipan. It had a woman's arm and most of her rib cage inside. They knew it was a woman because there was still fingernail polish on the fingernails. The shark's digestive juices hadn't got to the fingernails yet. We looked at the timing and figured what had happened. Not long before, two boatloads carrying two Saipan families had gone over to Tinian. They'd slaughtered a cow and taken the meat back on these little boats across the channel to Saipan. The boats flipped over with all this meat, and all the people were killed. The lady with the fingernails was one of them.*

For a time, McCoy was stationed in Yap, where he hung out with outer islanders, among them the shark people of Fais.

*We went out fishing once in Yap with my father-in-law and some other guys from Satawal,* he remembers. *We caught a seven-foot shark. I had these friends from Fais staying in Madrich, the little enclave where outer-island people stay in Yap, and I thought I ought to bring it in to them. So we came in with this white-tip on the bow of the boat.*

*The Fais guys grabbed the shark. They threw it over on a big pile of coconut husks by the Fais houses. That was Saturday night. Sunday morning, after church, here's this big shark still laying out in the sun, flies buzzing around. I said to these Fais guys, 'Hey, I thought you wanted that shark.'*

Carving of woman and crab, Yap,
Federated States of Micronesia.

Crab, Majuro reef,
Marshall Islands.

*'Oh, yeah, we do, but it's not ready yet. Don't worry, we'll eat it. We'll get to it pretty soon.' Those Fais guys were going to wait until she got really ripe, then cut her up. I couldn't get over it. The Satawalese guys just shook their heads.*

*People look down on the Fais people for eating shark. Everybody snickers at those people, but they're gutsy as hell for doing what they do.*

The Fais taste for shark developed of necessity. Fais is a small island with no lagoon. Fais fishermen have been forced to turn their attention to the open ocean and they have learned to like it. The Fais method is hair-raisingly simple. A Fais man swims out into the ocean pushing a boom or log. Attached to the log are lines, which the fisherman baits and drops. He attracts the sharks by splashing in the water. When the shark takes the bait, the fisherman pulls it up, lashes it to the log, and swims home.

\*     \*     \*

If the small, reef-poor island of Fais has an antipodes in Micronesia, it is the big, rich archipelago of Palau.

The Palau Islanders, 325 miles southwest of the Yapese, as fish scientists are as astute as their neighbors. Palau's varied landforms – volcanic, upraised limestone, and atoll formations – make a variety of substrates for marine life, and the islands lie close to a main dispersal line for Indo-Pacific marine forms. Palau's waters are the most biologically diverse in Micronesia, and Palau's folk scientists have risen to the occasion. Palauan natural history is oral. The unwritten *Ethnoichthyology of Palau* runs to many volumes.

As in Yap, marine biology is applied science in Palau, and here too it goes beyond what is purely practical to the fisherman. Palau's proverb-makers, subtle shapers of Palauan behavior and ethics, have built on their observations as fishermen.

*Like the octopus, able to change color*, goes one Palauan proverb, describing someone who is too adaptable.

*Like the 'meas' (a black reef fish), jumping into the net*, describes party-crashers and people who show up at feasts without invitations.

*Like one who has eaten the puffer fish – full of spines*, is an allusion to a big fish like the grouper, which sometimes finds itself in that predicament, and the proverb describes someone who has bitten off more than he can chew. (The English version is less humorous, it seems to me. It is certainly less pointed and sharp.)

*Like the eagle ray, eating while swimming*, describes rudeness, especially eating while walking, which is contrary to Palauan etiquette.

*Like the chambered nautilus, injured by one touch*, describes someone who is too thin skinned.

*Puffed out like a pufferfish*, describes a boastful person too full of himself.

*To make a minnow of a whale*, is to make a molehill out a mountain.

Sometimes the fisherman's observations, as worked over by the proverb-makers, go beyond even what is useful to the regulation of society and become poetry.

*Like the heart of the halfbeak*, Palauans say, describing a person as fancy-free as the miniature swordfish called a halfbeak is imagined to be.

*Like the man of Ngerechemai, who marked his fish traps with a cloud*, they say, describing a poor planner.

*A male child, though small, is like a young barracuda, bracing itself against the stream*, they say. The proverb depends on sharp observations of barracuda that have nothing to do with catching or eating that fish. Sharp-eyed Palauan fishermen saw young barracuda holding position against the flow of freshwater streams entering the lagoon. From time to time the barracuda darted forward, snapped up a small fish, then withdrew to its spot to wait for another. The fisherman liked that strategy and recommended it to boys. In Palau's competitive and often devious society, the barracuda's style of lethal watchfulness is good strategy indeed. The proverb is full of feeling, it seems to me, both for young boys and for young barracuda.

*Ngkora ngkelel aiusch el dimengel a medad rengii*, Palauans say. *Like a fish in deep, clear water, eaten only with the eyes.*

Palauan men hunt underwater with goggles or face masks and long wooden spear guns. The Palauan speargunner is patient underwater, as if he had all the time in the world down there; as if he had gills. Aiming, he steadies the five-foot-long wooden stock of his gun, then holds it rock still. His quarry turns tail several times in its hole in the coral, then pokes its head outside. The speargun discharges. The gun is so long, and the hand holding it so steady, so unalarming to the fish, that the range is usually point blank, a *coup de grace*. Instantly the metal spear shaft begins its rattling against the sides of the hole, as the fish inside thrashes. The magnifying effect of the water brings the death scene closer, but the water's muting effect moves that rattle off. The sound pricks the ear oddly; tinny and distant and staccato.

In shallow water, Palauan men armed with throwing spears pursue fish through the eelgrass. The spear shafts are wood, the tips three-pronged. This sort of hunting is good along the upraised coral-limestone coastlines of the hundreds of small southern islands Palauans call *elebacheb*, and in similar formations at the southern end of Babeldaob Island. The shores in those places are indented with coves, one small, roundish bay after another. At high tide, the spearman closes off the mouth of a cove with his net. He waits. When the tide is low, he douses his cigarette, takes up his trident, and wades after the fish trapped inside.

Palau's tidal fluctuations are the greatest in Micronesia. Aquamarine at high tide, the cove at low tide turns the color of its white-sand bottom. The spearman wades through the slick rubberiness of eelgrass, for this is the zone Palauans call *kosiil*, the eelgrass shallows. (*Like the eelgrass at 'kosiil', in with the tide and out with the tide*, Palauans say, of wishy-washy leaders.) The tide in the cove is now out, and the stalks of eelgrass all bend seaward. The fish flee from clump to clump, and the spearman cuts them down. His aim is uncanny. He almost never misses. As his eyes track the fish, his hand continually shifts position on the shaft. For deep-fleeing fish, his hand moves forward, the advanced grip giving his throw a deeper angle. For surface-fleeing fish, his hand moves back toward the butt. When the fish takes vigorous evasive action, the spearman's hand dances up and down the spear, like a violinist's along the neck of his instrument.

Hunting crabs in the mangrove swamp, a Palauan knows from the appearance of a mangrove crab's hole whether or not the hole is in use. He does not waste time on empty holes. The Palauan crabber knows also, from the color and consistency of the muck sealing an occupied hole, whether or not its owner is molting. If it is, he simply plunges his hand in and pulls the crab out. The great claws of a molting mangrove crab are soft and can't hurt him; using a spear then would only tear the crab apart. If the crab is not molting, the crabber uses his spear. There is no room for misinterpretation of crab holes, though, for a mangrove crab in full armor is the most formidable of crabs, and erring fingers get shorn off.

Off the southern island of Angaur, Palauan men fish deep water for the species they call 'oil fish.'

On the sand flats of Kayangel Atoll to the north, Palauan boys hunt sipunculid worms with their probing sticks and their worm-sensitive hands.

Palauan women hunt the reef everywhere for sea cucumbers and small fish. With old kitchen knives they dig for clams. I have tried my hand at clam-digging, swallowing my male pride. The women were amused at first, then instructive. They explained that I was to look for the 'eyes' of the clam, the siphons, and they showed me a pair of clam eyes so I would know how they looked. With a female Palauan finger pointing at them, the clam eyes were easy to see. Left to my own devices, I never saw another. In the time it took my companion to fill half her bucket, I had found one clam, and that one was by accident, and it was dead, besides – a gray, empty shell packed with sand.

In the murky water of the Ngersuul, a serpentine tidal river that winds its way through mangroves into the heart of Babeldaob Island, the women hunt clams with their feet. Their toes probe the muck, seize the clams prehensilely, and bring them up to the hands, which deposit them in buckets. The gray ooze of the riverbottom and mangrove riverbanks is hard to wash from clothes, so the women work naked. If a man chances to round the bend in a boat, the women run from the river or duck down in the water. There is a prank the Ngersuul women play, a prank as ancient as the river but one which always works. '*Ius*!' an old

Mother dugong (Cow fish) and her baby in Palau Reef. The dugong, a traditional delicacy in Palau, is now an endangered species and killing of the fish is forbidden.

Kite, Saipan,
Northern Mariana Islands.

woman will cry. Her sisters scatter, leaping for land. *Ius* in Palauan means crocodile. The saltwater crocodile, *Crocodylus porsus*, is one of the inhabitants of Palau's tidal rivers. Crying *ius* is not like crying wolf. '*Ius!*' is a false alarm that never fails to empty the river.

In Palau, as elsewhere in Micronesia, fishermen have a fondness for improbable tactics.

Palau's Southwest Islanders hunt needlefish aerially, with kites, and the craziness of that tickles not just the quasi-Palauans of the Southwest Islands, but all Palauans who have heard it.

The people of the Southwest Islands, besides dwelling on their own small, southwestern satellites of coral, live in an enclave on the volcanic islands of Malakal and Arakabesang, in Palau's central cluster, having settled there in numbers after typhoons hit their home islands early in the century. They brought their kite-fishing technique with them, and they practice it now in Palau proper. It is the only way to catch a needlefish, short of spearing one, for that elongated, excitable, gavial-beaked, good-tasting species won't take a hook.

The fisherman makes his *kedam*, or kite, from a breadfruit leaf. (*Kedam* is also the Palauan word for frigate bird, and it's a fine association, for the frigate, with its seven-foot wingspread and incommensurate body, is the supreme soarer in nature, capable of sailing for hours without a wingbeat.) After the fisherman has selected leaves for his kites and has set them to drying, he wanders the forest until he finds the web of a particular spider, a species known for the exceptionally sticky strands it spins. The fisherman forecloses on the web, rolling its strands into a ball, which he takes home with him. When his breadfruit leaves have sun-dried to a light-green, he builds kite frames of twigs. Each frame forces the ends of its leaf into an aerodynamic bow. Out on the water, sitting in his paddling canoe over a pile of leaf-kites, the fisherman picks one, and to its crosspiece of twigs he ties a kite string of sennit. He attaches a finer sennit string as the kite's tail. Onto the end of the tail he sticks a clump of spider web. He flies the kite out over the lagoon, bouncing the clump of web along the surface. The needlefish sees it, opens its long, baby-ichthyosaur's jaws, and strikes, entangling, in the web's stickiness, its fine and overabundant teeth. The fisherman pulls the kite in, trying to keep it clear of the water. He grabs the line and plays the fish to the boat.

Who were the brown Wright brothers who first dreamed that system up?

And why?

There are those, Mike McCoy among them, who think inventions like this were less the work of brown Wrights or Edisons than those of brown Rube Goldbergs. McCoy, who has seen kite-fishing elsewhere in Micronesia — it is a technique of the Southwest Islanders' cultural cousins in the outer islands of Yap and Truk — wonders sometimes why they bothered.

*In Satawal, they don't use spiderweb*, he says. *It's even more interesting. In Satawal they use the nerve ganglia in the lateral line of a shark. You catch a large, six- to eight-foot shark. You very carefully take out the nerve ganglia running along the lateral line — it's a big, white, long, sticky thing — and you use that as the tail of the kite. At least I'm assuming that's what it is — the ganglia. You catch small needlefish that way. They get their teeth caught in the ganglia.*

*Micronesian guys sit around and think these things up. I don't know. When you look at all the thought that goes into them, the amount of energy put in for the protein recovered, it doesn't make a lot of sense.*

But it makes a lot of sport, and it exercises the fishermanly inventiveness of Micronesians. Fooling around, they advance the state of their art.

In Palau, great fishermen become legends. A legend in his own time in Palau, and slightly before my time there, was Siakang. A big, powerfully muscled man, Siakang was a prodigious drinker and fighter and fisherman. I never met him, but I know his sister, Uldekl, who lives on Kayangel Atoll. If Siakang was a male version of that handsome, broad-shouldered, big-armed matron, then he was something to see.

Siakang's lung capacity astounded Eugenie Clark, early in the career of that marine biologist and diver, before she went on to fame herself. One of Siakang's methods for spearing fish, she reports, was to seize a stone for ballast, dive 15 or 20 feet to the reef front, grip the coral with his feet, and wait. This was before the vogue of spear-guns, and Siakang used a hand-spear. Anchored to the reef, he held it poised. He did not believe in pursuing reef fish; he waited for them to come to him. Slowly the fish overcame their fright at his arrival. They poked their heads tentatively out of crannies in the coral, ventured forth, dashed back in. Reassured that nothing bad had happened, they ventured out again. They swam in curiosity towards the new fixture on their reef.

Siakang had a trick he liked to play on newcomers ignorant of his reputation. He played it once on Eugenie Clark. He played it again on Robert Owen.

Bob Owen spent 30 years in Micronesia, first as Chief Entomologist for the Trust Territory, then as Chief Conservationist. Early in his own career, Owen went diving with Siakang, unaware that the Palauan was superhuman underwater. Siakang free-dove to 50 feet, Owen estimates, and began working at a giant clam with his knife. As Owen watched from the surface, the great vise of the shell seemed to close on Siakang's arm. Siakang yanked desperately at the arm and gestured up. Owen dove. He was unable to get down to Siakang's head before his air grew short and he had to return to the top. Getting his breath for a second dive, his chest aching, Owen looked down, and he saw Siakang detach his arm. The Palauan swam upward, grinning. (Owen did not know, then, that all those hand-trapped-in-giant-clam tales of the Pacific are myths — a giant clam cannot close tightly enough to trap a human.) After a few hours, Owen says, he was able to appreciate the humor in the stunt.

Siakang's death was fitting. At a picnic at which he and everyone else was drunk, he dived after a sea turtle and did not come up. His companions sobered up enough to dive for him, but no one could go deep like Siakang, and they never found him.

The end may not have been the end, of course.

With a man like Siakang, the absence of a corpse leaves room for doubt. Maybe Siakang is still pursuing the sea turtle. Maybe he is simply avoiding his wife. She is said to have nagged him a lot — with every reason, probably — but Siakang may have lost patience with it. He may have preferred the company of fishes, with whom he had more in common, anyway. Maybe he lurks around down

there, playing the longest breath-holding prank of his career — someday to surface once more.

\*  \*  \*

Planners for Micronesia's future, noting the excellence of the islands' fishermen and the heavy concentrations of tuna in Micronesia's offshore waters, have long hoped that a commercial fishery — offshore tuna boats manned by Micronesians — would be the way to lead the islanders into the 20th century and out of the welfare state. Through most of the 1970s, everyone in Micronesia was cheery about the prospects for Micronesians fishing tuna. No one is cheery that way any longer. The emphasis now in the governments of Palau, the Marshalls, and the Federated States of Micronesia (Yap, Truk, Ponape, and Kosrae), is in getting the best possible licensing fees from the foreign tuna fleets that fish here.

Mike McCoy was one of the principals in trying to get a Micronesian tuna fishery started.

*Van Camp has a cannery in Palau*, he says. *Bob Carpenter of Van Camp tried to get Micronesians fishing. When I was in Yap, I used to send a lot of outer-island fishermen down to him. There was a boat of fishermen from Ponape. A boat of Trukese. A boat of outer islanders from Yap. We were really trying to do it. It just didn't work out.*

*This was when the Koreans first started getting into tuna fishing, in '75 or '76. The Koreans came down with four boats. The crew was taxicab drivers, assembly plant workers, farmers. They didn't know anything about fishing. They had a couple of captains that were long-line captains, not tuna fishermen. A guy I know from Satawal was detailed for two months to teach one of these Korean captains how to fish for skipjack. In six weeks, the Korean captain was outfishing the Micronesians. His crew worked every day. They didn't get drunk on weekends. They showed up. They kept going.*

The explanation one hears most often for Micronesian reluctance to fish offshore is that Micronesians are traditionally reef and inshore fishermen. Their distaste for offshore fishing is cultural. McCoy does not buy that:

*It's got nothing to do with deep water. It's just a hard life. You're away from your family all the time. Who needs it? Micronesians don't need it, not*

Dolphin motif, men's house, Yap,
Federated States of Micronesia.

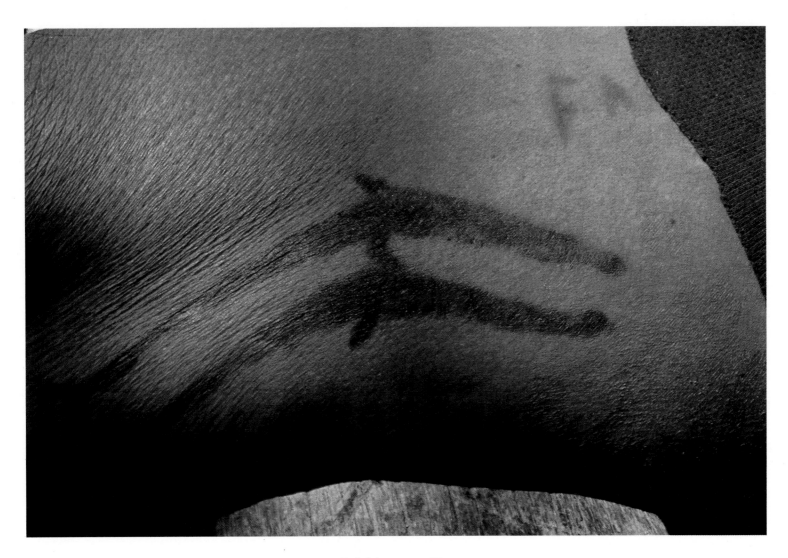

Dolphin tattoo, Yap,
Federated States of Micronesia.

*with the $60 million a year that Uncle Sam puts in here. The alternative for those guys from Korea was probably sleeping in a doorway. Micronesians don't have to do that.*

*I had a 53-foot boat in Yap. We were reef-fishing in Ngulu and Ulithi. For every 20 crew members, I found, you get about five good ones. It's like in any society — you have to look at the odds. In Japan you have 100 million people, and you get 10,000 skipjack fishermen. In Micronesia you get 100,000 people you're probably going to find 100 skipjack fishermen. It's probably about the same ratio.*

One hundred skipjack fishermen, obviously, are not enough to put a dent in the skipjack resources of Micronesia's hundreds of thousands of square miles of territorial waters.

*In the mid-'60s, you might have had a chance, says McCoy. You could have gathered the information on the resource; you could have built an infrastructure — roads, docks, slipways. They were never built. When I was in marine resources at Yap, we got $750 every three months to develop fisheries. Now it's too late. The technology is advancing so fast, Micronesians will have a hell of a time catching up. I think it's out of the question. No one in the Federated States of Micronesia is talking about that anymore.*

McCoy stops. He thinks for a moment. He seems to change direction.

*If people here want to get organized, it's going to be a real uphill struggle, he says. If you paint a picture of a vast area with untapped resources that will solve everyone's problems, you do Micronesians a real disservice. If you go to the other extreme, and say this is the Sahara Desert of the Pacific, and there's nothing here, and the people are destined to live forever on food stamps, you're also doing them a disservice. The truth is somewhere in between. There's enough to make it, but they've got to get their noses to the grindstone and start doing something. It's not India, for Chrissake. It's not Bangladesh.*

*There's a bunch of good Kapingamarangi guys just down the road. They don't mind going out, getting wet. There's good guys from the outer islands of Yap . . .*

The tuna-fishing dream dies hard, even in Mike McCoy.

A logical alternative, should offshore fishing by Micronesians prove unfeasible, might seem to be a commercial reef fishery. There is a problem, though, with making money from the reef: the resource is relatively small and fragile, and the markets are distant. McCoy is one fisheries specialist who feels that way. *You don't want to commercialize reef areas*, he says. *A place like Pingelap, for example, has maybe three linear miles of reef. That's enough for the people there, but not enough for export. There are a few areas, way off the beaten track, with good potential for commercializing – Ngulu, say, and Minto Reef – but there aren't many.*

Not everyone agrees. In 1975 I traveled to Kayangel Atoll, Palau with a local Palau fisheries officer, a young American eager to persuade the Kayangelese to go into reef fishing as a business. I sat with him one evening on the plank floor of the young people's meeting house, listening as he spun out his plans for regular visits by a freezer ship and his predictions of the money that could be made. I liked him. He was earnest and seemed truly concerned with the welfare of Palauans. I thought he was crazy. My sentiments were McCoy's even then.

Cash is poisonous to subsistence economy. The snake in tropical Eden, to be as colorful as I can, is green and forms an S. When a fisherman hunts a reef for food for his family, he stops when he has speared enough. Fishing for subsistence, he is more careful about maintaining the reef as a renewable resource than when he fishes for export. The reason, I suppose, is that the subsistence fisherman is under no delusion that there's any other kind of wealth.

The fisheries man couldn't *promise* the ship, he said, but he was reasonably sure of it. All he needed was some manifestation of interest by the fishermen of Kayangel.

His audience was 10 or a dozen Kayangel men. They sat with their backs against the meeting house wall, some staring blankly at a spot several feet above the fisheries man, some even higher, up into the meeting-house rafters. Two men fell asleep. They were weary, I imagine, from a full day of fishing.

The fisheries officer was a redhead, and his face flamed with the sunburn of the long boat trip up. By the end of the meeting, that red burned deeper with disappointment. I don't know whether that blankness of his audience lay in the belief, shared with me, that commercialization was wrong for their reef; or that the Kayangelese, who live healthily and well on $80 a year per capita, saw no need to break the bank; or that they didn't believe in the 40-acres-and-a-mule promise of the freezer ship; or that they were simply fatigued. They asked one or two questions, from politeness, then lapsed into a boredom they made no effort to conceal. The meeting ended, the two sleeping men woke, the Kayangelese filed out. Yusim, the school principal who had served as translator, thanked the fisheries man for his visit. The fisheries man looked wildly from Yusim to me, I think for support. My face too, I'm afraid, was blank.

The best thing for the Micronesian reef, it seems obvious, would be continued management according to the home-grown ecological principles that have succeeded in maintaining, through generations of Micronesians, for a millennium or two, a rich and healthy reef. The reef-management principles of Europe, or the absence of any, in just a century or two have succeeded in destroying or impoverishing coral reef all over the Pacific.

Of course, nothing in those old management principles tells a Micronesian how to buy the new outboard engine he sees in the catalog or the new radio.

Micronesians are good, but not perfect stewards of their reef.

*There's only half a square mile of reef on Satawal*, says Mike McCoy, of his sometimes home. *Satawal is poor in reef fish. The people are very, very conscious of the limitations on that reef. Taboos close off portions of reef in certain seasons. For the past eight months, it's been taboo to use a spear on the reef. And sometimes they ban nets.*

*At the same time, there's an amazing amount of ignorance. I did a study of the turtles on West Fayu, the turtle island where the Satawalese sail for turtles, and I was surprised. The Satawalese were killing turtles before they spawned. They didn't know the gestation period of the eggs. They gave me estimates of anywhere from eight to 80 days. They didn't know how many times each female came in to lay, and what the interval was. They're not quite so sharp about those things as the Palauans, who know a tremendous lot about how the reef works.*

Yet even the Palauans, careful reef scientists that they are, have fallen considerably from the ecological equilibrium of the past. The newer generations of Palauans are no longer guided by the

Tridacna, giant clam in Palau Reefs, Palau,
Republic of Belau.

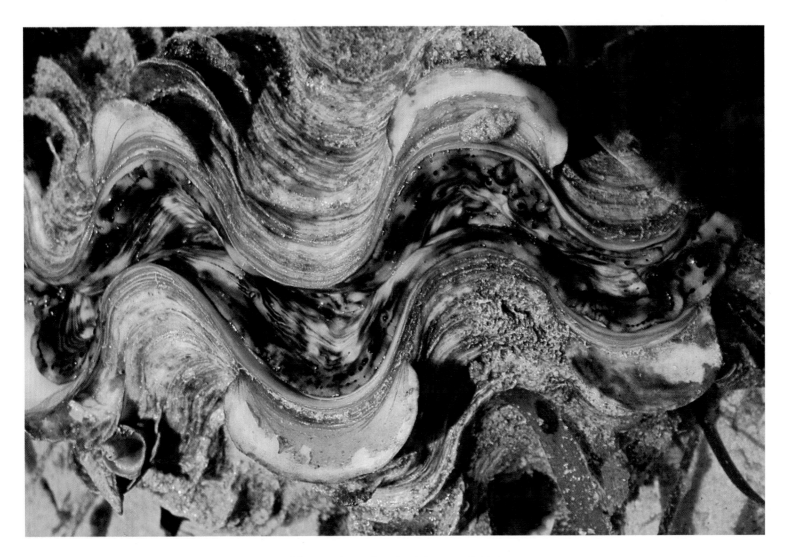

Tridacna, giant clam in Palau Reefs, Palau,
Republic of Belau.

concept of *kerreomel*, the conservation ethic of Palau's old days. Many young Palauans have not even heard the word. Palauans with scuba gear now travel to the deep passes in the reef where giant grouper breed and speargun them in the spawning season. In those fishermen, the old Palauan competitiveness, the ethic that makes Palauans a race of over-achievers, is no longer balanced by the ethic of *kerreomel*. Killing gravid fish in breeding season is the kind of shortsighted, cash-inspired enterprise not tolerated in traditional times. The question, as always in these matters, is whether the new equipment is responsible, or the liberation from an old ethic. The answer, as always, is probably a little of both.

There are Palauans today who hunt the easy way, poisoning fish with Clorox and dynamiting them. In Palau, as elsewhere in Micronesia, fish-bombing became a problem in the postwar years, as islanders became expert at defusing wartime bombs and shells and extracting the explosive. One result has been a lot of one-eyed men with missing fingers. Another has been acres and acres of dead reef. Bombing kills not just the present generation of fish, edible or not, but the coral upon which future fish generations must depend.

The stories about fish-bombing that make the rounds in Palau should serve to limit the practice, but they don't seem to.

Shortly after the war, one story goes, a Palauan man extracted explosives from a bomb and fashioned himself some grenades, which he rigged with homemade fuses. Armed like a Marine, he set off in his boat. Approaching what looked like a sea turtle, he lit a fuse and tossed a grenade. As it left his hand, he took a closer look. He wished with all his being that he could call his grenade back. The turtle was a naval mine. The fisherman turned his boat to flee, planning to leave the scene horizontally; instead, he left vertically, riding a tremendous explosion. He lost some fingers, but the rest of him is still alive, and you can see him around today.

Another time a Palauan was fishing with grenades from a sheer, jungle-covered cliff in the *elebacheb* islands. He saw a school of rabbitfish directly below him. He cocked his arm, but saw no opening in the vines and tree trunks through which to toss. Maneuvering a little, he found a triangular gap in the branches. It looked big enough, and he tossed. The grenade hit a branch and bounced back at his feet. The fisherman jumped. He went crashing through the vines and branches, just ahead of the blast, and he hit the water, joining the rabbitfish, who were surprised to see him.

I like to think that this fisherman, as he floated, his ears ringing from the blast, his body scratched by vines, the twigs and dust and gravel raining down on him from the cliff, the rabbitfish gone, might have seen the error of his ways. Perhaps he did, but the lesson hasn't taken, and now and again in Palau one hears a distant boom from the reef.

Before contact with Europe, Micronesians had impact on their reefs, of course. No system of taboos and prohibitions could protect a reef entirely from fishermen as accomplished as the Micronesians. It was not a virgin reef that they passed from generation to generation.

Pristine reefs do exist in Micronesia, uninhabited places, examples of what the Pacific must have been like before human beings of any sort ventured out in it. One such place is Helen Reef, southwest of Palau. Another is Bokar Atoll in the Marshalls. Bill Pululoa has visited Bokar. When the days of sailing ended in the Marshalls, Bokar ceased to be called upon, and so far as Pululoa knows, his visit, on a bait survey, was the first in 40 years.

*The lagoon is full of sharks, but they don't bother you,* he says. *On the lagoon bottom we saw these big coral heads. After a while, we noticed that they seemed to be following the boat. When the boat would stop, they would stop. They were big humphead wrasse. You couldn't throw a lure overboard without instantly catching a fish. Big jacks were biting the props. One sheared the pin. We landed and we looked around. As you walked along the beach, fish in the lagoon would follow you. When you stopped, they stopped.*

But we don't miss what we don't know, and few of us have known places like Bokar. Coral reef as maintained by Micronesia's traditional fishermen is as populous and colorful an ecosystem as anyone could reasonably ask for. It continues to feed Micronesians, and that is the real test.

The reef of Guam, the island where Western civilization has been established longest in Micronesia, is depauperate. Guam's reef could not begin to feed the people there. The trouble is not simply in the density of Guam's population. Micronesia's traditional system handled heavy populations well. Yap, before contact with Western diseases, had 50,000 people. Now there are 5,000. Palau had from 50,000 to 70,000 inhabitants, and now has around 15,000. And yet, by all accounts, both of these archipelagos had more fish in the old days. Whatever the Micronesians were doing, they were doing it right.

Mike McCoy, having grumbled about the Satawalese for taking female turtles, concedes that, *Generally, the turtle taboos in the Carolines worked. Margie Falanruw believes that the introduction of Western religion meant the biggest trouble for the reef. She thinks we've got to find a substitute for that old system of taboos, and I think she's right.*

Margie Falanruw is a botanist from Yap who, with McCoy and her husband Sam, co-founded the Yap Institute of Natural Sciences. At marine-resources conferences outside Micronesia, McCoy and Mrs. Falanruw like wearing their 'Yap Institute of Natural Sciences' pins, which confuse the other delegates, few of whom have heard of Yap.

When I visited the tiny one-room building that houses Mrs. Falanruw's institute on Yap, she told me that she hoped the old taboos could be 'neo-traditionalized.'

That, she admitted, would not be an easy undertaking.

It was the old Palauan artist Charles Gibbons who first told me of the concept of *kerreomel*. It was, he said, a *good* concept. Gibbons's English is weak, and I sensed more weight in his 'good' than that word was really intended to carry. *Kerreomel*, he said, meant the wise use of things — land, food, gear, wildlife — so that they would last. Contemplating *kerreomel*, Gibbons smiled a wistful smile.

The trick will be to neo-traditionalize the old system while there are still elders around who remember what it is.

Shoal of fish, Yap,
Federated States of Micronesia.

Fishing for damselfish, Yap,
Federated States of Micronesia.

# Ruins

The thunderhead rose like a Greek column from the flatness of the sea. Its capital was a gigantic, billowy mountain of cumulus, its shaft a nearly solid curtain of rain. In relation to that column, our plane was a dust mote. Our altitude was about four-fifths of the way up the shaft, our bearing straight toward its center.

The plane was an old twin-engine Beechcraft with a long, unattractive nose. It comprised the entire fleet of PMA, Pacific Missionary Airlines, and it was the one aircraft serving the State of Kosrae of the Federated States of Micronesia. The baggage compartment that occupied the long nose was full of spools of wire, suitcases, and cardboard boxes bound with tape and addressed in felt pen to various sisters, mothers, and cousins on Kosrae. I sat in the co-pilot's seat wearing headphones. The view was good, but I would have preferred sitting back in the cabin with the half-dozen Kosraeans returning home. When the pilot suffered his heart attack or stroke, I would simply die. My life would pass before my eyes without commercial interruption – no nagging distraction of wondering whether I should be doing something. In the beginning, I had carefully watched the pilot to see if I could get the hang of flying. I had made a half-hearted attempt to study the needles in all the dials.

The needle of my own courage stood at seven-eighths full. I was mildly hungover. I had drunk one beer too many at my hotel the night before, or the barmaid had played *Coward of the County* on the jukebox a few too many times.

I wished this weren't an airline run by *missionaries*. The missionary-pilot did his own engine work. I prayed that he got truly greasy in that engine, that he didn't simply trust in the Lord to keep him aloft.

The gray metal of the instrument panel was worn silver in places. The panel ended below the windshield in a shelf, which someone had carpeted long ago. The carpeting was ratty, now.

The pilot, Peter, wore shorts and old Nike running shoes. His accent was American, with a trace of his native German. His hair had been bleached white-blond by the tropical sun, and his legs were tanned, lean, and muscular. It looked as if he really *ran* in those running shoes. Jogging, I knew, took dedication in the humidity of the tropics, under the puzzled or amused brown eyes of native islanders. Running missionaries did not have to battle hangovers, I supposed, but I was impressed just the same. More than that, I was relieved. Peter was fit. His cardiovascular system was in working order. That was good.

The rain shaft of the thunderhead now filled the entire windshield. The first raindrops hit the glass, multiplied, and then the world was obliterated in a tropical torrent. The water found a seam in the windshield and began dripping steadily on my knee.

For a while we traveled in whiteness. The rainstorm was like that featureless fog of the *Mr. Jordan* movie where Claude Rains plays the urban angel-host on a liner whose passengers don't realize yet they are all dead. But we came out alive on the other side. Ahead, across 50 miles of ocean, another pillar of rain made its way toward us, and beyond it a host of pillars. If the storm behind was a Greek column, then ahead the Pacific was a parthenon.

On the floor between Peter's seat and mine was his thermos of coffee. He unscrewed the cup and we took turns drinking. It was bad coffee, but sipping it, my courage, in anticipation of soon returning, actually began to return.

Peter pointed. Through a break in the clouds to our left an atoll was making a misty appearance.

*Pingelap*, he said over the headset. We watched the atoll's island get bigger, and Peter spoke again into his mike. *Ten percent of the population of Pingelap suffers from eye disorders. They have cataracts. They're supersensitive to the light. It's sad. You see kids running around squinting all the time. It's incest, you know.*

Inbreeding was the better word, I suppose, and Peter was reporting only the dark side — or in this case, the bright side — of the story. I had heard the other side from a resident of the atoll of Mokil. *The Pingelapese are really good at night*, the Mokilese had said. *They see real well at night, fishing.* I was glad that the affected Pingelapese had that compensation; otherwise their malady, here in this brightest region on earth, would have seemed too cruel.

Two and a half hours after our departure from Ponape, the island of Kosrae appeared in the clouds ahead. At first it seemed to levitate, a gray mountain-island in the sky. At the speed of the Beechcraft, the island took forever getting closer. Then we passed some critical point; Kosrae rapidly got larger, and its gray became green. The island moved down from its spot in the sky and became an island in the sea. The jungly, precipitous ridgelines that many consider to be the most beautiful terrain in Micronesia took shape. From our angle of approach, the mountain jungles appeared virginal and unbroken. The beach of white sand that rimmed the island was unmarred by jetty or pier. I could see no sign of Kosrae's ruins. Kosrae looked little like the seat of a former empire.

\*   \*   \*

There is on Kosrae a ruined city of basalt. To newcomers that usually comes as a surprise. The world is familiar with the thatched roofs of the Pacific, the grass dresses, the sennit fishlines, the carved wooden masks. That Pacific Islanders built permanently and grandly in stone does not fit our idea of the Pacific's material culture. But the tumbled stones of the Kosrae ruins, overgrown by jungle, are not the only such stones in Micronesia. On several of the islands of the Marianas group lie *latte* stones, coral-limestone pillars which, with their huge rounded capstones in place, once supported the great houses of the Chamorros. In Palau, rising from the savannah grass in the Ngerchelong District of Babeldoab Island, is a double row of dark monoliths said to have been columns for a dwelling. The Palauans called the place *House of the Giants*. The ruins of Yap are more modest, yet more ubiquitous. The Yapese ruins don't suggest a grander past, just a more populous one. Everywhere in Yap stand stone house platforms empty of houses. Everywhere fitted-stone paths run from deserted village to deserted village. All the inhabited islands of the Pacific suffered depopulation after contact with Europeans and their diseases, but the depopulation of Yap is studied today as a classic case. There once were 10 times as many Yapese as the 5,000 that inhabit the archipelago today. Here and there among the empty house platforms is a platform still alive with a house — the dwelling of survivors.

Nan Madol ruins, Ponape,
Federated States of Micronesia.

"House of the Giants," Ngerchelong, Palau,
Republic of Belau.

The most famous of the Micronesian ruins is Nan Madol, on Ponape. The site is at the edge of a mangrove forest, behind man-made seawalls, overlooking the Pacific. The architecture of Nan Madol's central palace, or temple, looks vaguely Mayan, vaguely Cambodian, vaguely something unidentifiable. The high walls are built of long, massive basalt blocks. Broad, gentle-sloping staircases lead into an interior divided by lesser walls, and within the lesser walls are mounds, platforms, and occasionally, sunk in the stone pavement, odd rectangular crypts. Nan Madol is thought to have been built by the same people who earlier had built the city on Kosrae, which in many of its features Nan Madol resembles. The legend is that the Kosraeans once conquered and ruled Ponape and parts of Truk. Ponape's Nan Madol, like the earlier city on Kosrae, was never finished. Bad luck dogged the race of architects who built the two cities, or something pursued them, for their fate was always to move on before they were able to complete their walls.

From the ground, when my plane landed, Kosrae looked nothing at all like a fallen Rome. The only ruins I could see were recent ones. The runway was a short stretch of gravelly blacktop, an angled spur on the causeway that joined the small capital island of Lelu to Kosrae's mainland. The service road alongside the runway had become a Hall of Ruined Vehicles. The shells of old trucks and tractors lined the road on either side, making hummocks in the wall of vines that overgrew them and bound them together. There was a school bus, painted yellow, its engine cavity empty. There was a yellow Dodge truck with *Trust Territory of the Pacific Islands/Kosrae* stenciled on the door. Two cranes at the end of the line appeared to be alive still, but the plugs of all the others had long since given up the spark.

Inland, the mountains were sheer yet so densely covered with vegetation that none of the underlying rock or soil was visible. Above the point where the causeway met the main island stood two hills in the shape of mountains. At the crest of each, a final spray of vegetation bent away from the sea wind, like spindrift blowing off the top of a steep green wave.

As we drove along the causeway to Lelu, my driver asked that in a minute, once we passed some intervening trees, I look inland at the central ridgeline and tell him what I saw.

*A reclining woman?* I guessed instantly.

He glanced at me sharply, suspicious, I think, that I possessed unnatural powers, or that I had lied about never having visited Kosrae before. It was neither of those things. It was just that he had happened to touch on one of the few anthropological theories of any significance that I have ever advanced – a theory which, until that moment, had been latent and unformed. Only with the driver's question had it come clear for me. It was this: that to all peoples, all mountain ridgelines look like reclining women. If my theory is sound, and I am confident that it is not, then this tendency to see ridgelines as reclining women, along with the taboo against incest, are the only universal human traits. Thus the ridgeline is the original Rorschach test.

We came out from behind the trees, and I saw the reclining woman. She really did look like a reclining woman, much more than, say, Tamalpais, the California mountain which to the early Spaniards had seemed to resemble a reclining woman and under which I grew up. Kosrae's reclining woman has an unattractive face, big and craggy, but her breasts are firm and conical.

*She's pregnant,* I said. The driver nodded and told me the myth of how the mountainous spine of Kosrae had come to be pregnant.

Kosrae is thought to be one of the centers from which proto-Micronesians dispersed through the rest of their islands. This may be so. It is hard to believe, though, from the look of the place, that anyone would ever want to leave. Kosrae is a lovely island, prosperous and self-contained. It is fertile land, an island of farmers, a place famous throughout Micronesia for its limes.

It is a land of images, such as these:

*A boy walking along the causeway from Lelu, bound for the family farm. His gait is slightly asymmetrical, for one foot is bare and the other wears a zori. The waist of his trousers is overample, and a two-inch band of underwear shows above. He has removed his shirt and rigged it as a sling for the machete on his shoulder. Inland, puffs and wisps of mist linger everywhere on the high slopes, as if some early-morning fairy arsonist has*

*preceded the boy up there. To his left, a flock of shorebirds make pinpoint landings on the blacktop of the airfield, wasting almost all of the runway's length. They stand in a group and watch him pass.*

*A sudden lizard on the windshield of your battered rental Toyota. The smack of its falling is loud for the lizard's weight but the lizard is uninjured, apparently. It's a puzzled bit of life spilled off by the vegetation overhanging the road, as if the Kosraean jungle could hold no more biota and this lizard were the excess.*

*Cats and dogs everywhere in town; the former pets, the latter sometimes dinner.*

*A fruit bat hovering in the blue sky between palm crowns, its doglike chin tucked into its breast as it looks down on you. In Kosrae, fruit bats are plentiful and fearless, for they, unlike Kosrae's dogs, are not eaten by the human inhabitants. Elsewhere in Micronesia, where bats are a delicacy, they are more leary, and it is strange to see one so close and curious. The bat looks as improbable as one of those hybrids of medieval lore – half fox and half raven. Its wings are two feet across. It's a little funny and a little scary, like Bela Lugosi. Its curiosity satisfied – having visually drunk its fill of you – the bat banks up and away, disappearing over the palms.*

*Women and girls in flower-print dresses of Dayglo colors. Never a woman or girl in jeans or shorts, for Kosrae, of all Micronesia's islands, is the one on which Christian missionaries left their mark most indelibly. Kosrae is one of the more remote islands in Micronesia's remote sea, and in its isolation Kosrae's Christian notions about dress have remained old-fashioned. Above the knees in Kosrae, the legs of women are religious mysteries. Their backs are no secrets at all. To get comfortable in the heat of Kosrae, the women reach back and unzip their dresses down to the waists.*

\*     \*     \*

I had been in Kosrae for just two days when, in spite of myself, I felt a new anthropological theory coming on. The theory was outlandish, and I tried to suppress it. It began in my impression, as I listened to Kosraean – one of the more anomalous in Micronesia's family of languages – that it was inflected

Sokehs Rock, Ponape,
Federated States of Micronesia.

Reclining Woman, Kosrae,
Federated States of Micronesia.

suspiciously like *Chinese*. Any linguist could have put that suspicion instantly to rest, surely, but no linguists were available.

There was another thing. The Kosraeans did not tuck their dead away in cemeteries. They kept them close to home. In many of Kosrae's yards stood stone grave markers in the shape of churches – white, peak-roofed slabs with crosses at the heads. The crosses were usually heaped with fresh-cut flowers. They were well maintained, but not subject to any stiff sort of veneration. Occasionally I saw a child sitting on one. My first thought was, How civilized! Continental Christianity's practice of segregating its dead in huge tomb-reservations seemed unfriendly by comparison. In Kosrae, a child playing in his front yard could rest comfortably for a moment on his grandmother or grandfather. My second thought was, How oriental! Kosraeans kept their predecessors handy in small shrines. Their custom smacked of ancestor worship.

There was a third thing: the ruined city. I had not seen the ruins yet, but their high walls, like those of Nan Madol, were said to be upturned at the corners, a configuration that strikes many observers of both cities as looking vaguely oriental; as resembling, somewhat, the upturned corners of pagoda roofs.

As a joke on myself, I shared my theory with Sterling Skilling, the Kosraean who manages the island's bulk oil plant, and with Thurston Siba, Kosrae's postmaster and one of its principal businessmen. The three of us were sitting in a restaurant on Lelu. Kosrae's language, I proposed, was descended from the Chinese. The island was settled by passengers from some ancient, storm-blown junk, thus the burial customs on the island and certain details of the architecture.

That was a new theory on him, Sterling Skilling admitted. He smiled and shook his head, but, for a moment at least, he seemed willing to consider the possibility. His native language, he agreed, was a weird one, structured nothing like the languages around it. It did sound sort of Chinese.

Thurston Siba said nothing. He gave me a look that I chose to regard as thoughtful.

Neither man *looked* the least bit Chinese, I had to concede, but

that proved nothing. Sterling's last name, Skilling, was American. He was descended from a 19th-century American sailor, though his Malayo-Polynesian features gave little hint of that. The genes of my Chinese castaways had many hundreds of years in which to be drowned in the Malayo-Polynesian tide.

The next morning we were having breakfast in the same restaurant. It is, so far as I know, the only restaurant in Kosrae. It is owned, I believe, by Thurston Siba; it shares, at any rate, the building that houses Thurston's general store. Its prices are the most reasonable in all Micronesia. Coffee costs a dime. Sterling and I sat with the Kosraean who is in charge of historic preservation on Kosrae, and we discussed the island's ruins. The ruin site was called *Saru* in Kosraean, I learned. The word was pronounced more like 'shareh.' It was not a proper name – the site did not have one. *Saru* meant simply 'ruins.' According to the historic-preservation man, an archaeologist was scheduled to come out soon for some serious digging; at the moment, though, the restoration program was very modest, mostly just an attempt to arrest any further decay in the stone walls.

Thurston Siba, who had been listening from a far table, called over. If I explored the ruins, he said, I would find small vaults here and there. In the old days, people who disobeyed the king were buried alive in the vaults.

The historic-preservation man nodded. According to Kosraean lore, he said, the ancient city was built by ghosts. Not long ago, an old man had seen a ghost at the site. The ghost was not translucent, nor did it have any kind of aura. It looked just like a mortal man. It wore a thu and a very long beard.

Then the historic-preservation man told me, in afterthought, that bad things happened to outsiders who trespassed in the ruins. He instantly looked embarrassed, either by the superstition or by the inhospitality of his island's ghosts.

*They say it was built by ghosts,* he said, *but I believe it was people. Most of the ruins are basalt, but there is a lot of coral, too. I believe they used the coral rocks to build an incline and rolled the basalt blocks up that. The walls were unfinished when the people left, so there's coral all over the place.*

The ruins, I assumed, were deep in the boondocks, reachable

only after a long tramp through the jungle. I supposed that now I would have to go find them, and I wondered whether you could drive close by road. That road was sure to be potholed. Would Thurston, from whom I was renting an old Toyota, let me take the car on a trip like that?

*How do you get to the ruins?* I asked.

*Walk across the street*, Thurston said. *See that building? Go past the end and look through the trees. You'll see the first wall.*

The ruins, it turned out, were all around. If, earlier, I had peered a little harder into Lelu's dense green, I would have seen them. The ancient city had covered the entire island of Lelu. Today, in an age less grand, Lelu was the smallest of towns, bustling, in the sleepiest of ways, only along the road that rimmed the island.

They showed me a map. It was entitled '*Die Ruinen Von Kusae*,' and it had been drawn by a German archaeologist named Paul Hambruch in 1910. I puzzled for a moment over the legends. A real Oceanic anthropologist, as opposed to an imitation one like me, has to read German, for ethnologists and archaeologists from Germany did most of the important early work in this part of the Pacific. I tried to fake my way through Hambruch's map. The *Mabstab* – the 'map-scale,' for those of you who don't read German – was 1:2000. *Basaltmauern* was easy, too. These were walls of basalt, indicated on the map by a heavy black line, and they composed the heart of the city. *Korallensteinmauern* were walls of coral stone, and they were by far the more extensive. In the old days, coralline walls partitioned the island of Lelu from shore to shore. The causeway from Lelu to Kosrae's mainland had been there back in 1910. The map showed that the rest of the city had contained a complex of a size and intricacy difficult to connect with the green, overgrown Lelu of today. There were sea walls then where none exist now. Artificial channels penetrated the island all the way to the high basalt walls of the central city.

I decided that on Sunday I would explore the ruins. On that day I would be alone. As nearly as I could tell, I was the only heathen on the island. Saturdays on Kosrae were spent, by everyone but me, in preparations for Sunday, and Sunday was spent in church.

With no humans to interrogate, I would interview silent stone.

Saturday night it rained.

At nightfall, thunder began to roll and lightning to flash, and that continued all night long. At about two in the morning, one bolt seemed to hit the house. The flash lit the insides of my eyelids, dazzling me, and the roll of thunder was instantaneous and tremendous. It was like dreaming Hiroshima. I got up and looked out my second-floor window. Across the street, the sign above Thurston Siba's general store was scarcely visible through the rain. The street lamp beside the store illuminated a sphere of the storm. The lamp looked as if it were burning inside a waterfall.

I was living in Thurston's house. For Micronesia, the house was huge. The second floor had been partitioned into five or six rooms for Thurston's older boys and for roomers like me. The rooms were bare except for a bed or a sleeping mat. There were no dressers; Micronesians tend to keep their clothes in suitcases tucked under the bed. There was a common room with a balcony that looked across to the store and a bookcase in which every one of the books was Christian and inspirational. One title, *The Dust of Death*, looked as if it might be different, but it proved, on my opening it, to be more of the same.

I walked quietly downstairs. The linoleum floor down there was vast and empty of furniture, except for one sofa. In daytime, that vastness of linoleum and absence of furniture always looked strange to me; tonight it looked surreal. Sprawled, as usual, on the plain of linoleum squares where sleep had overtaken them, positioned like pieces in some outsized game nearing conclusion, were several small children and two teen-age boys. Some of the children slept on mats, some did not. Kosrae's night temperatures are so warm, even in rainstorms, that Kosrae's mothers do not worry unduly about lack of sleeping mats. They see nothing wrong, either, in a child's sleeping in his clothes. The identity of the children on Thurston's floor seemed to change from night to night. I had never learned Kosrae's kinship system; I did not know whether these children were all part of an extended family or just playmates who happened to be at Thurston's when sleep struck. Tonight, with each lightning flash, their recumbent shadows leapt

Detail, Storyboard, Palau,
Republic of Belau.

Detail, Storyboard, Palau,
Republic of Belau.

across the floor. They did not stir. For Kosrae's children, apparently, the thunder is a lullaby. A few consecutive days of cloudless blue sky would set Kosraean children to crying, I suppose, and cause frightened Kosraean dogs to jump underneath the bed.

Impressed by the example of the children, I went back upstairs and slept.

When I woke again after daylight, it was to the normal Kosraean alarms: roosters and dogfights. The rain had stopped, and calm lakes and pools stood everywhere in the street. Women in bright Sunday dresses and men in Sunday shirts were already beginning to stream north, threading their way through the lakes and pools. They might have been some antediluvian folk bound festively, through drowning streets, to an ark. They were, in fact, Christian soldiers bound for church.

Joining the brightly dressed stream, I accompanied it for 50 yards. A careful observer might have spotted me as the stranger in this crowd. I was Caucasian and eight inches taller than the average Kosraean adult, of course, but aside from that *I was the only one barefoot*. After last night's deluge, I anticipated a lot of wading. I was interested, besides, in recording whatever anthropological messages the bare stones of the ruins, by their temperatures or textures, might send me through the soles of my feet. A quarter mile from church, I ducked into the trees.

Wading through a shallow swamp that yesterday had been a lawn, I saw the first low wall. Its stones were of gray-black basalt and they were huge. The wall reminded me a bit of the fitted-stone walls of the Incas, had those been transported somehow from the thin air of the Andes down to a dim and humid tropical forest at sea level.

The long blocks of basalt were naturally faceted. They would have been cylinders, had they not spalled themselves away cleanly, on several sides, along their entire lengths, so that when seen end-on they made polygons. The walls were built in layers, one row of blocks laid at right angles to the row below it, a stratum of polygons alternating with a stratum laid longitudinally. I climbed the first low wall, and beyond it was a higher one.

Following this second wall to its corner, I stopped. There, 20 feet above my head, the top of the wall had a vaguely oriental, pagodalike upward turn, with a final post of basalt protruding like a bowsprit. That highest block must have weighed a ton. The lowest block, the massive cornerstone directly under it, must have weighed 20. I asked myself the question that modern man always asks, when confronting ancient ruins: *How did they move those stones?*

A cobbled pavement of coral ran alongside the wall. I followed it until I came to a break in the wall – a former gate, I guessed. Looking in, I saw that the walls formed a rectangle, enclosing an area about the size of a football field. Whatever it was that the interior of the high-walled compound had held originally, it was planted now to banana trees.

The walls themselves were overgrown in places by small banyans. The trunks and branches of the trees were buttressed by slender aerial roots, which clutched and tendriled the stones.

The cobbled pavement of corals became a path, and the path led off into the forest. I followed. My feet had learned after 10 steps or so which corals made the best footing. They knew to avoid the dark corals, which tended to be sharp. They picked their way along the whitish corals, which had slightly raised, striated, or labyrinthine surface patterns that felt pleasant underfoot and kept my feet from slipping. Descending a slight incline, the cobbled path became a stream. The day was warm already, and the slight, cool current of the rain-fed stream felt good.

I must have been in the middle of the old city, now, but the forest had closed behind me, and I saw no trace of ruins. Vegetation rioted, or at least it conducted a spirited demonstration. There were giant breadfruit trees. There were spindly young breadfruit waiting for a break in the canopy so they could grow to the light. There were old coconut palms carpeted with epiphytes two-thirds of the way to their tops. Birds called in the forest. It began lightly to rain.

A second stream joined the first, and soon I was wading mid-calf through a clearwater swamp of nipah palms.

I lost touch with the path. I could no longer feel the cobbling of coral underfoot; it had been replaced by the fine, firm mud of the swamp floor. I continued in the same general direction, and soon my feet found the stones again. The path led me out of the water and into the ruins once more.

Emerging from the nipahs, the path passed narrowly between two broad, 30-foot-tall mounds. The mounds were artificial domes of coral built atop a foundation of basalt. I started up the dome to my left. The coral stones that surfaced it were the same species that composed the path, and my feet followed the whitish corals to the top. Whatever purpose the mound had served originally, it was now a fortress of lizards – blue-tailed skinks, which scattered before me as I climbed. At the summit was a sort of crypt, a rectangular well framed in dark basalt and sunk in the lighter-colored corals. The crypt was half full of rainwater, and circles of new raindrops were spreading there. As my head topped the rise, something under water in the crypt saw me and scuttled away to hide under a rock. A crab, I thought at first, before remembering that this water was fresh. Some kind of gigantic water beetle?

I remembered what Thurston Siba had said: that ancient kings had sealed disobedient subjects in these crypts alive. Maybe this creature of the pool was one of those rebellious spirits reincarnate.

I spent the rest of the morning exploring the ruins. They seemed to go on forever. Whenever I thought I had seen the last wall, a fork in the path that I had overlooked before would lead me to a new one. I found several more mounds with crypts on top, some full of rainwater, some dry and full of leaves. The coral rubble was everywhere. I remembered the speculation of the historic-preservation man – that his ancestors had used the coral to build inclines up which to slide the basalt blocks. In some places the coral did shore up unfinished walls, as if providing an incline indeed had been the purpose, but in other places, as on the mounds and at the tops of high walls, it seemed the wrong explanation. Maybe the builders simply liked the look of caps of coral on their mounds and walls. Or maybe the successors to the builders, a folk less skilled as engineers, had used coral to repair the walls, having lost the techniques to manage basalt.

The blue-tailed skinks were everywhere. They were the ancient city's 20th-century inhabitants. Whenever I walked along

Turtle rock imprint, Yap,
Federated States of Micronesia.

Men's house, Yap,
Federated States of Micronesia.

the walls — high walls and low, finished and unfinished — those cobalt-blue tails flicked as the lizards retreated from me. A safe distance away, the tail would flick again as the lizard stopped, cocked its head, and looked back. I found myself indulging a fantasy: that the original inhabitants had worn long, cobalt-blue loincloths.

At the edges of the ruins, prehistory and the present overlapped. In one deep garden abutting the ruins, the owner had built a pig pen against the basalt, incorporating the ancient wall. At the margins of the ruins, gardeners used the walls for fences; the land within several of the high-walled compounds was planted to bananas, or to breadfruit, or to taro. Chickens wandered the outskirts of the ruins. Walking along the top of one marginal wall, I saw two hens hunting and pecking along the top of the next. The hens spotted me, saw that we would meet in the corner, and hopped down, yielding the wall to me. In places along the outermost walls, I found caches of empty beer cans, mostly the big heavy-gauge cans of Foster's, a good Australian import. Kosraean boys must go down to the ruins to drink, just as Southern boys go down to the levee.

I liked this overlap of ages. I found I preferred my ruins this way. Better the jungle, small stashes of beer cans, and a few foraging chickens, than a weeded, sanitized place entirely dead.

Emerging from one thicket, my skin wet from the rain and from its damp-brushing by tropical leaves, I looked down to see a tiny, delicately whorled snail crawling on my arm. It seemed a friendly gesture by the forest. That the snail could have mistaken me for vegetation made me feel less a trespasser here, and it lifted some of the curse from the Curse of the Ruins. I had never really believed the legend that fate punished outsiders who intruded here, but all ruins are haunted places, and the confidence of the snail laid most of that hauntedness to rest.

I came to the very middle of the ruins. If not the geographical center, I decided, then this spot was the heart. It was a place where two of the high-walled basalt compounds met, sharing a common corner. From out of that nexus grew an enormous banyan. The tree's size was impossible, magical. Its dark canopy spread like a thundercloud, its curtains of aerial roots made an entire forest of their own.

Flowing along the base of one basalt wall, as if from a spring under the banyan, was a sort of stream-pool, a clear, broad, inch-deep sheet of water. I stepped in, planning to wade to the tree. I expected the black mud at the bottom to be firm, as it had been in the nipah swamp. My feet plunged in, the memory of the curse leapt up, and my hand grabbed for the cool stone of the wall. I sank to mid-thigh before I stopped. My feet had encountered nothing solid; only the tensile strength of the mud arrested me. The black ooze of fertility here seemed bottomless. Beyond, growing from the stream-pool, in the angle where the two walls met, was the biggest swamp taro I had ever seen. It had leaves like green sails, and its tubers would have fed a battalion.

I was not ready to turn back. The deep mud blocked my passage along the bottom of the wall, so I decided to walk the top. I would climb around, or through the banyan.

From a distance, it appeared that the great tree and its clusters of aerials had obliterated the wall, but on drawing close, I saw that the roots, instead of tumbling the stones, had bound them together. All the basalt blocks were in place. If something there is that does not love a wall and wants it down, then something there also is that likes a wall and holds it up. Tree and basalt were hopelessly intertwined, the banyan a part of the wall, the wall a part of the banyan. Half rock-climbing, half tree-climbing, I threaded my way through the aerial roots and came out on the other side.

Nothing bad had happened. If the curse was going to strike, it seemed to me, it would have been during my passage through the banyan. The Curse of Saru may be a delayed one, of course, like King Tut's, but as of this writing, three months later, nothing bad has happened yet.

I could look down, now, into the adjacent compound. In places free of rubble, the compound floor was planted to dryland taro. A blue-tailed skink fled ahead of me along the wall, then hid, foolishly, in a shallow depression in the stone. I covered the mouth of the depression with my hand. It was almost as if the lizard had wanted to be captured. I brought it out gently and admired that cobalt-blue tail.

Sitting on the wall, just beyond the shadow of the banyan, with the skink in my hand for company, I rested. I thought about the people who had built this place. What were they like? How had they moved stones? Why had they abandoned their city, leaving it unfinished? Where had they gone?

If there was a lesson in the ruins, it seemed to me, it was the lesson of all ruins: Empires Don't Last.

I released my skink. The blue tail flicked off along the wall. A safe distance away, the lizard stopped, cocked its head, and looked humorously back at me. Then the tail flicked again and disappeared.

World War II Japanese Zero fighter plane at Yap Airport, Yap,
Federated States of Micronesia.

U.S. World War II tank at the Saipan beach front, Saipan,
Northern Mariana Islands.

# Epilogue

The Guam Hilton overlooks a large, shallow bay on Guam's west coast. Close inshore, running across the mouth of the bay, is the barrier reef. From what the hotel calls its 'Tree Bar,' a guest can watch the long lines of breakers curl in against the reef. The Tree Bar is not like a tree house; its stools are on the ground. The bar makes a circle around the tree, and the bartenders work with their back to the trunk. There is an opening in the circular roof to allow for the exit of the tree's branches.

The island of Guam, for anyone concerned with the future of Micronesia, comes inevitably to represent one possible avenue into that future. For me the Tree Bar came to serve as a convenient abbreviation of that symbol.

Guam has flawlessly paved roads and boulevards, not the potholed tracks that pass for roads on most Micronesian islands. On Guam everyone drives a car, has modern medical attention, watches television, reads a daily paper. Guam is United States Territory, and in Guam's stores one can buy any game or gadget or appliance, and almost any book, that one can buy on the American mainland. There are multi-storied tourist hotels. There are tree bars. There are shopping malls, power plants, gas stations. There's a moribund, or at least depauperate, reef.

Toward the end of my stay in Micronesia, I found myself at the Tree Bar. It was mid-afternoon, not a drinking hour. Besides my friend and me, there were only three drinkers at the bar, and none of us was serious. A small placard before us advertised two of the house specialties. One side showed 'the Blue Pacific,' an aquamarine-colored drink. The other side showed 'the Tropical Itch,' which was pink or rash-colored. I don't remember what I was drinking, but it was neither of those. Looking through the center of the bar's circle, past the tree and the bartender, I could see the deck chairs arrayed in ranks on the green Astroturf beside the pool. Stairs from the bar led to the beach below, down to a line of red-striped beach umbrellas, and more deck chairs. The deck chairs of both levels were occupied almost entirely by Japanese.

Most Americans cannot afford the prices at the Guam Hilton. Empires don't last forever, as the ruins at Kosrae had testified, and the American economic empire at the moment was in decline. The Japanese empire, which three decades before, beginning with military defeats in these very islands – Saipan, Pelelieu, Truk – had received such a disastrous blow, was presently waxing again. Most of the Japanese were young honeymooners, and the skin of most was white. Tonight it would be bright red, except for the lines left by wristwatches and halter straps.

In one of the chairs lay a middle-aged American woman whom I saw there for hours every day. Her skin was crustacean-colored – not the scarlet of a boiled lobster, but the dull iron-red of a cooked mangrove crab. I wondered if any of the Carolinian navigators, brown-black men accustomed to sailing for a week in the sun, could take the amount of ultraviolet that this dedicated woman had conditioned her skin to take.

My drinking companion, it happened, was the first modern white man to accompany Carolinians on a long voyage in an outrigger canoe. His name is Carlos Viti, and in 1972 he sailed with the great navigator Ikuliman from Puluwat to Guam. The canoe was named *Santiago* and it was the first outrigger in this century to make that crossing. Viti and the others ate turtle eggs throughout the trip. At night they rubbed coconut oil over their bodies to fight the cold. In one storm, they chanted to an effigy kept in the navigator's hut. Sailing out of the 15th century, they arrived at 20th-century Guam after dark at a spot not far from where Viti and I now drank. The first man they saw was a Guamanian nightfishing with a flashlight on the reef. The canoe slipped up on the fisherman silently, and somebody on the canoe said, *Hello*. The fisherman, who had thought he was alone on the reef, jumped. He admitted later that he thought he'd heard ghosts.

Carlos Viti first came to Micronesia in 1967 to work as a Peace Corps Volunteer in the lower Mortlock Islands, a remote place where the traditional life is strong. He remained in Micronesia and became a photographer. His assignments in the islands are seldom to document Micronesia's future, since that is unformed and unphotogenic. He photographs canoes, old chiefs, tattoos – the Micronesian subjects that at present have all the character. Viti lives now on Guam, but he is more a man of Micronesia's past.

*I remember my first canoe house*, he was saying. *The canoe inside – it looked like a museum piece. It was like finding a dinosaur or a pterodactyl that had somehow survived. I used to get in these time warps, sitting alone in the canoe house under one of these voyaging canoes. The end products of thousands of years of trial and error. What about all the designs that failed? Then Ikuliman walks in wearing his* thu. *The ancient race. The anachronism.*

A short time later we were still speaking of canoes – my notebook was open before me – when one of those anachronisms came toward us, wading through the shallow water just off the beach below.

It was a Chamorro net-fisherman. His casting net draped over one shoulder, he was walking the slow-motion walk of all net-fishermen, sliding his feet forward in a way that did not disturb the surface, his eyes fixed on the shallows. Now and again he would freeze in mid-stride and stand staring at the water. Net-fishermen need sharp eyes. The sardine schools that they pursue show only as subtle ripplings and dimplings of the surface, or as multiple quick-shifting shadows on the sand bottom. After a minute or two, the net-fisherman would move a little, and the slow-motion walk would resume. His was the glacial, stalking stride, the unblinking stare, of a wading bird. It was, I thought, almost as if this human had slipped into the spirit of a heron. Except it wasn't that – it wasn't imitation. It was convergent evolution. This was how a bipedal animal walked when its food was sardines.

It occurred to me that in few particulars did this fisherman resemble the Chamorros who had worked this beach in 1520, before Magellan. This net-fisherman, and all other modern Guamanians, were as much Spanish, Filipino, and Portuguese as they were Chamorro; in color, stature, and style of thought they made a new race. Only the heron eyes were the same.

The fisherman passed below. At his back, 10 feet away, were the red-and-white-striped beach umbrellas and the pale Japanese in deck chairs; and on the lawn above, more ranks of pale Japanese in deck chairs, and the iron-colored woman, and the pool, and the Astroturf, and the Tree Bar. None of it seemed to exist for the fisherman. His entire being was auxiliary to his eyes, right now. He was in another universe.

*They have star tracks to islands that aren't even there any more, Carlos*

Viti was saying, of his Carolinian navigators. The emphasis was his, and I underlined the words in my notebook. *They have* myths *about why those places aren't there any more. It's eerie. They knew all the passes in the reef on Guam, though they'd never been there. Those guys are the real thing. They are* the men. *And there's nothing like it left.*

I jotted this down, too. Looking up from the notebook, I saw that the net-fisherman had stopped again in mid-stride. He was balanced lightly on his trailing foot, like a heron on one leg. An infinitesimal shift in the net on his shoulder, or something in his posture, told me the sardine school had turned his way and was very close.

Watching the fisherman, I changed my opinion. In some compartment of his mind, I realized, he must be aware of the beach umbrellas behind him. He must know about the pale Japanese, the deck chairs, the Astroturf, the Tree Bar, Carlos Viti, and me. With eyes like his, he had to feel all our eyes behind him. I had a new fancy. The fisherman, stalking the school, frozen on that back foot, was simultaneously stalking the civilization behind him.

Civilizations don't last forever, as Kosrae's ruins had attested.

I remembered other net-fishermen I had seen in other Micronesian ruins. In Palau, I had watched an old man cast his net from one of the ramps of the long-abandoned seaplane base on Arakabesang Island. The seaplane base had been built by the Empire of Japan. The imperial concrete runways were pocked with craters from American bombs, and scrub vegetation had reclaimed most of the rest. And in Yap I had watched boys with casting nets walk along the tumbled stones of one of the Yapese fish weirs that point, like gigantic Von Daniken arrows, toward the sea from which the ancestors of the Yapese came.

It was not hard to imagine this Chamorro net-fisherman casting his net off the ruins of the present civilization. Lately the indications had been multiplying – fuel shortages, inner-city decay, the spread of terrorism – that this civilization might not be immortal, either.

Carlos Viti had said *anachronism*, and of course he was right. But the word means simply 'out of time.' It says nothing about whether the proper time is past or future.

It was possible, I thought, that the time warps Viti entered in the canoe houses of Puluwat did not run backwards, as he imagined. It was possible that the Chamorro net-fisherman was slow-striding out of the 21st century, not the 15th. Carolinian navigators and Chamorro net-fishermen run not on oil or uranium, but on their wits. They have lasted out empires before.

Whichever era the net-fisherman hailed from, I was glad he was here. It was reassuring that human eyes still knew how to become a heron's, that human arms could still send out a casting net in a perfect circle on the sea.

Text © Kenneth Brower
Photographs by Harri Peccinotti
Editor: Gregory Vitiello
Art director & designer: Derek Birdsall
Production: Martin Lee
Typesetting by Balding & Mansell
Printed in Singapore by Tien Wah Press (Pte.) Ltd.

Published 1981 by Louisiana State University Press,
Baton Rouge, Louisiana 70803

ISBN 0-8071-0992-4
Brower, MICRONESIA          LC# 81–82822

Gregory Vitiello of Mobil selected our theme – Micronesians and the sea – and he picked Harri Peccinotti and me to tell the story. Harri and I are grateful to Mobil Oil Micronesia, Inc. for sending us through Micronesia and for supporting us there during the three and a half man-months that the note- and picture-taking required. For their help in the islands, we are grateful to J.P.Bailleux, Alex V.S.Shaw, H.L.Tarkong, Charlie Gibbons, Thurston Siba, Tony DeBrum, Anna Maria Adelbai, Bob and Hera Owen, John Koichi, Bill Pululoa, and Pedro Harris.

We are also grateful to Mobil bulk plant supervisors Justino Ramon, Hilario Bermanis, Billy Jonas, Sterling Skilling, Orlando DeBrum and Fermin Bultedaob for their assistance and guidance.

The chapter on canoes owes many of its facts to *Canoes of Oceania*, Vol I, by James Hornell, and to the Palau Community Action Agency's *A History of Palau*, edited by Kathryn Kesolei. The chapter on navigators borrows from the research of Thomas Gladwin in his *East is a Big Bird*, and David Lewis in *We, the Navigators* and *The Voyaging Stars*. The story of the 1970 voyage of the brothers Repunglug and Repunglap of Satawal is based on an account by Michael McCoy. Most of the Palauan proverbs herein were collected by Robert McKnight in his *Proverbs of Palau*. Almost all the information on the ethno-ichthyology of Yap was lifted from an unpublished undergraduate paper by Margie Falanruw of Yap, which is the only written discussion anywhere of that vast and labyrinthine subject.

*Kenneth Brower*

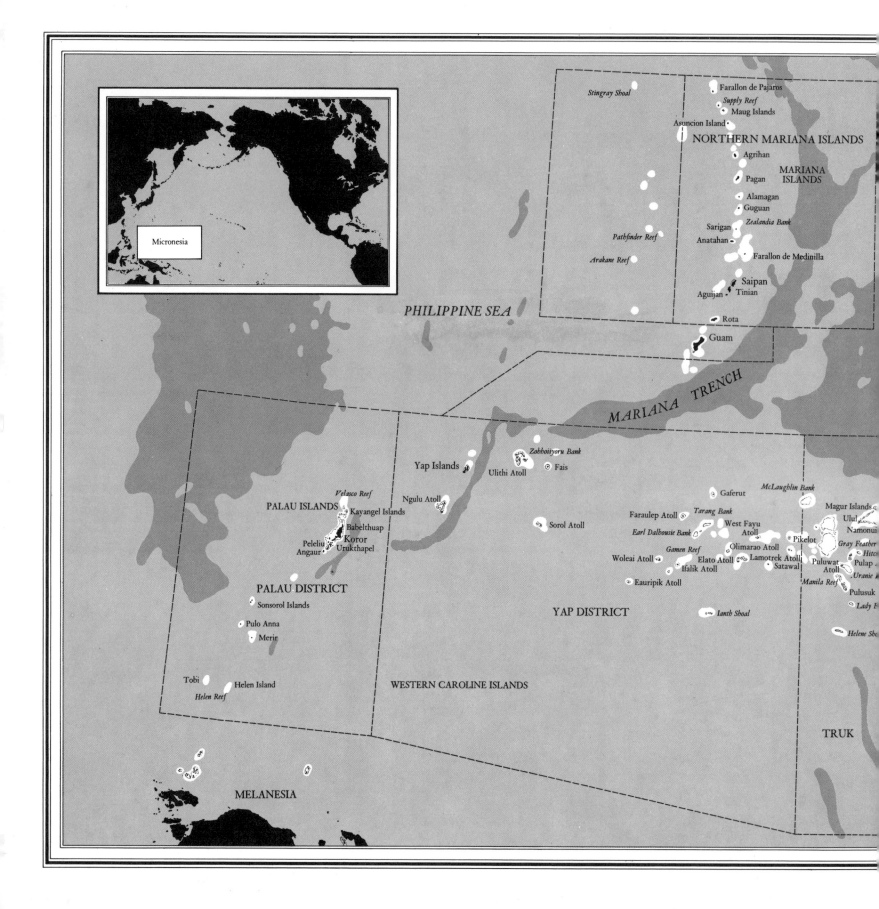

Micronesia

Stingray Shoal

Farallon de Pajaros
Supply Reef
Maug Islands
Asuncion Island

NORTHERN MARIANA ISLANDS

Agrihan

MARIANA
ISLANDS

Pagan

Alamagan
Guguan

Zealandia Bank

Sarigan
Pathfinder Reef
Anatahan

Arakane Reef

Farallon de Medinilla

Saipan
Aguijan   Tinian

PHILIPPINE SEA

Rota

Guam

MARIANA TRENCH

Yap Islands

Zohhoiiyoru Bank

Ulithi Atoll   Fais

Ngulu Atoll

Gaferut   McLaughlin Bank

Magur Islands

Velasco Reef

PALAU ISLANDS

Kayangel Islands

Faraulep Atoll   Tarang Bank

West Fayu
Atoll

Ulul
Namonui

Sorol Atoll

Earl Dalhousie Bank

Pikelot   Gray Feather

Babelthuap

Peleliu   Koror
Angaur   Urukthapel

Gamen Reef   Olimarao Atoll

Lamotrek Atoll

Puluwat

Hiten

Pulap
Atoll

Woleai Atoll

Elato Atoll
Ifalik Atoll

Satawal

Uranie

PALAU DISTRICT

Manila Reef

Pulusuk

Sonsorol Islands

Eauripik Atoll

YAP DISTRICT

Ianth Shoal

Lady F

Pulo Anna

Merir

Helene Sho

Tobi   Helen Island

Helen Reef

WESTERN CAROLINE ISLANDS

TRUK

MELANESIA